NICOLSON VC

Peter D. Mason

Geerings of Ashford Ltd.

First published in 1991 by
Geerings of Ashford Limited,
Cobbs Wood House, Chart Road, Ashford, Kent.

Copyright © P. D. Mason, 1991

All rights reserved. No part of this publication may be reproduced, stored in a retrieval system, or transmitted, in any form or by any means, electronic, mechanical, photocopying, recording, or otherwise, without the prior permission in writing of the publishers.

Every effort has been made by the editor and the publishers to trace holders of copyright material.

Photoset in 10/11 pt Times Roman and printed by Geerings of Ashford Ltd., Ashford, Kent, England.

ISBN 0 9513042 9 1

THE LIFE AND TIMES
JAMES BRINDLEY NICOLSON VC DFC RAF

CONTENTS

Prologue — based on his personal account of the action leading to the award of the Victoria Cross ix

Acknowledgments v

Bibliography vi

Foreword — by Group Captain Leonard Cheshire VC OM DSO and 2 bars, DFC RAF viii

1 Early life — education — apprenticeship — call to the colours — No 10 FTS 1

2 Posting to RAF Church Fenton — No 72 Squadron —courtship and marriage — personal narratives by squadron colleagues — 'the wager' 9

3 Service with No 249 Squadron — early wartime operations — personal reminiscences of squadron members 31

4 The Victoria Cross — the Air Ministry decision — feted by Kirkby Wharfe and York — the Investiture at Buckingham Palace 51

5 Posting to No 54 Operational Training Unit and the Turbinlite Flight — Leeds Warship Week 71

6 The Burma Campaign — the background —operational conditions — the formation of No 27 (Flying Elephants) Squadron . . . 77

7 Nick — and the 'Flying Elephants' —operational sorties —train 'busters' — reminiscences and narratives by members of No 27 Squadron — the award of the Distinguished Flying Cross 87

8 Transfer to HQ, 3rd Tactical Air Force and HQ Royal Air Force, Bengal — involvement with No 355 (Liberator) Squadron —the last flight to Rangoon — recollections by a survivor —the Singapore War Memorial 117

9 Brickbats and bouquets — tributes and remembrances —the Nicolson Drive — about Muriel Nicolson 126

Record of Service — the Official Roll 139

Aircraft Flown 151

DEDICATION

Our thoughts go back to our unforgettable experience of the Battle of Britain —when day by day we saw the strange and dreadful conflict fought out far up in the skies, and night by night awaited the news of the number of aircraft, theirs and ours, destroyed.

For three months, England, our enemies and the world hung upon the actions of these young men, and of their comrades, who made and serviced the machines in which they fought. It seemed then, as it seems now, that they stood alone between us —and the abyss.

The Archbishop of Canterbury at the
Dedication of the Royal Air Force Chapel
in Westminster Abbey, 10 July, 1947

ACKNOWLEDGMENTS

It is with grateful thanks that I acknowledge the many kind and generous contributors, the world over, who have unstintingly given of their time to record impressions and recollections of half a century ago, not an easy task as the memory dims with the relentless and uncompromising passage of time.

Perhaps one person who may be an exception to the general rule is Mrs Muriel Nicolson, whose memory is still acutely accurate for dates, events and personalities. She has contributed a wealth of detail for her husband's biography and without whose full support and approval, giving authenticity and an inner dimension, would not have been possible. Her photographic and documentary assistance has greatly enriched the content of these pages.

My thanks go out to other gracious contributors, from Air Rank to Aircraftsman who shared experiences with James Nicolson, in peace and in war, in the conviviality of the mess, and at the height of danger and adversity.

I am indebted to Group Captain Leonard Cheshire VC OM DSO DFC who took the time from his heavy schedule of work in order to write the foreword for this biography. I warmly acknowledge the assistance and narrative given by James Nicolson's former Squadron Commanders, Marshal of the Royal Air Force, Sir John Grandy GCB GCVO KBE DSO, and Air Chief Marshal Sir Ronald Lees, KCB CBE DFC, for their specialised reports and comments.

PHOTOGRAPHIC ACKNOWLEDGMENTS

The sources of illustrations, maps and documents are many and varied. Suffice it to say that all items are warmly acknowledged, some never having been published before.

BBC Sound Archives

BIBLIOGRAPHY

The author extends his grateful thanks to the following for their kind contribution, use of material and advice in the compilation of the biography.

'Gun button to Fire' .... Wing Commander T F Neil (William Kimber 1987)
'Beaufighters over Burma' .... David J Innes (Blandford Press 1985)
'That Eternal Summer' .... Ralph Barker (Collins 1990)
'The Flying Elephants' .... Chaz Bowyer (William Kimber 1965)
'Flying Made My Arms Ache' .... Wing Commander 'Wally' Wallens (Self Publishing Ass'n Ltd)
'The Spitfire Summer' .... Peter Haining (W H Allen 1990)
'Fighting Church Fenton' .... P D Mason (Pegasus Studio 1989)
The Royal Air Force 1939-1945 (Volume 3)
Hilary St. George Saunders (HMSO)
'The Sky Belongs to Them' .... Dr. Roland Winfield (William Kimber 1976)
'The Battle of Britain — Then and Now — . Winston G Ramsey (After The Battle publications)

Mr Andrew Saunders — Curator, Tangmere Military Aviation Museum
Simon W Parry (Air Research Publications) in association with Flypast magazine.
Adur District Council
The Controller — H.M. Stationery Office and Public Records Office, Kew.
Mr A C White — The Spitfire Society
The Hon. Secretary and members — 355/356 Squadron Reunions
Aircraft and Aircraft Experimental Establishment — Royal Air Force, Boscombe Down.
No. 72 Squadron — Royal Air Force, Aldergrove, Northern Ireland.
No. 27 Squadron — Royal Air Force, Marham.

Photographic Appreciations

The Controller — H.M. Stationery Office.
Keeper of Photographs — Imperial War Museum.
The Royal Air Force Museum — Hendon.
The Ministry of Defence.
Commonwealth War Graves Commission, Maidenhead.
The Daily Express.
Mr W H(Bill) Hughes, Group Captain D F B Sheen and Wing Commander F M Smith (ex. No. 72 Squadron)
Mrs Jeanne Baines (nee Nicolson)
Mr Alex Dinwoodie and Mr Edgar Welch (ex. No. 27 Squadron).
Air Photo Supply and Air Portraits.
Wing Commander T F Neil (Ex. No. 249 Squadron).
Mr Trevor Williams, Mr Andrew Saunders, Mr Eric Kightley and other members of No. 355 Squadron
Mrs Muriel Nicolson.
Others not mentioned are warmly acknowledged.

EVERY EFFORT HAS BEEN MADE TO TRACE HOLDERS OF COPYRIGHT MATERIAL

Group Captain Leonard Cheshire VC OM DSO DFC.

FOREWORD

by

GROUP CAPTAIN LEONARD CHESHIRE
VC, OM, DSO and 2 bars, DFC

My recollections of James Nicolson are restricted to the week or so we spent together at the Viceregal Lodge, Calcutta, in September 1944.

Both of us, I suspect, were a little out of our element, I more than Nick, since I had only recently arrived from the European theatre, whereas he had been based in India and Burma for some time, as I recall it.

This probably threw us together in a special way, and we had many talks on both life in general and the operating aspect of air-warfare in that part of the world. He, of course, was a fighter pilot whereas I was a bomber pilot, but not knowing exactly what my duties were to be until I reached Headquarters 224 Group I wanted to learn as much as possible.

Nick had one of those personalities that makes one feel drawn to him and at ease. He also had a special brand of humour which I found very appealing. He was a legend to us wartime pilots, the only fighter pilot VC which he earned during the Battle of Britain — just two months after I had begun my own operational career. Moreover, he stood out as someone quite exceptional; there seemed to be a certain parallel between the action that gained him his award and his determination once out in India to leave his desk and get back to operational flying. A man whose aircraft was on fire, who was already severely burned himself, on the point of evacuating his aircraft and then, because he unexpectedly saw an enemy aircraft in his gunsights could drop back into the seat and continue firing until the enemy aircraft was out of action clearly stands head and shoulders above the ordinary pilot.

A topic that we discussed in detail was the role of the Mosquito in the Far East theatre. The Mossie was the queen of the wartime aircraft, and for me had been the key to accurate marking for the high level precision bombing technique that was needed in order to destroy the V2's. But, because it was a wooden aircraft one suspected that there would be problems in a hot climate with the glue joints, which ultimately proved to be the case. However, in the meantime I hoped to make the most of them if I had any say in their use and Nick was the ideal man to consult.

Sadly, though, it was this determination to get to grips with the enemy that led to his tragic death, as was the case with Guy Gibson.

Had we, the older pilots of 617 Squadron, still been there at the time, we would never have allowed Gibson to fly, for the reason that he was at a desk, and therefore did not have his hand in. But Guy, like Nick, waited his opportunity, and talked his way into something that should never have been allowed.

There is a saying 'As a man lives, so he dies'. This was true of Nick, as it was of Guy . . .

London. 1990 — *LEONARD CHESHIRE*

NICOLSON VC

or

The Life and Times
James Brindley Nicolson VC DFC RAF

PROLOGUE

16 August, 1940. It was a glorious day, the sun was shining from a cloudless sky, and there was hardly a breath of wind anywhere.

Our Squadron was heading towards Southampton on patrol from Boscombe Down flying at 15000 feet when I observed three Junkers 88 bombers about four miles away, moving across our bows. I reported this to our Flight Commander, and he replied —'go after them with your section'. Breaking away from the Flight, I led my section of three Hurricanes round towards the bombers and chased hard after them, but when we were about a mile behind I saw the 88s fly straight into a squadron of Spitfires. I used to fly Spitfires myself and I guessed it was 'curtains' for the Junkers. I was right, and they were all shot down in quick time, with no pickings for us! I must confess that this was very disappointing since I had never fired at a Hun in my life and was longing to have a crack at them. So we swung round again and started to climb to 18000′ over Southampton to rejoin the squadron. Our section was still a long way from them when suddenly, very close and in rapid succession, I heard four bangs, the loudest that I have ever heard. They were made by four cannon shells from a Messerschmitt 110 which hit my machine. The first shell tore through the hood of the cockpit, sending splinters into my left eye, one splinter I discovered later almost severed my eyelid. I couldn't see through the eye for blood. The second cannon shell hit the spare petrol tank, setting it on fire, whilst the third shell crashed into the cockpit and tore off my right trouser leg. The fourth shell struck the back of my left shoe, shattering the heel and making quite a mess of my foot, but I didn't know anything about that either until later.

The instantaneous effect of the shells was to make me dive away to the left in order to avoid further enemy action, then I started to curse myself for my carelessness. I thought, what a fool!!

I was thinking of abandoning the aircraft when suddenly a Messerschmitt 110 whizzed underneath me, in full view of my gunsight. Fortunately, no damage to my windscreen and foresights, so I began to chase the 110, setting everything for a fight. When the Hun was in range I pressed the gun-button, he was taking violent evasive action by twisting and turning to get away from my gunfire so I pushed the throttle wide open. Both of us must have been doing about 400 as we went down together in a dive. First he turned left, then right, then left again, finally turning right. I remember shouting loudly at him when I first saw him — 'I'll teach you some manners, you Hun' — and I shouted other things as well! I knew that I was scoring hits on him all the time I was firing, and by this time it was pretty hot in the cockpit from the effect of the burst petrol tank. I couldn't see much flame but I knew that it was there alright. I remember once looking at my left hand which was keeping the throttle open, it seemed to be on fire itself and I could see the skin peeling off it yet I could feel little pain. Unconsciously I had drawn up my feet under my parachute on the seat — to escape the heat I suppose. Well, I gave the hun all I had and the last I saw of him was when he was going down with his left wing lower than the right one, and I gave him a parting burst.

As he disappeared I then started thinking about saving myself and decided that it was about time that I abandoned the aircraft and baled out, so I immediately jumped out of my seat but hit my head on the framework of the hood which was all that was left. I again cursed myself for a fool and pulled the hood back — and wasn't I relieved ! It slid back beautifully. I jumped up again, but again I bounced back into my seat for I had forgotten to undo the straps holding me in. One of them snapped so I had only three to undo, and I left the machine.

I suppose that I was about 12-15000 feet when I baled out and immediately started somersaulting downwards, and after a few turns like that I found myself diving headfirst for the ground. After a second or two of this I pulled the parachute ripcord, the result was that I immediately straightened up and began to float down.

Then an aircraft, a Messerschmitt I was later told, came tearing past me and I decided to pretend that I was dead by hanging limply on the straps. The Messerschmitt came back once more and I kept my eye closed but I didn't get the bullets that I was half expecting. I don't know if he fired at me, the main thing is that I wasn't hit . Whilst descending I had a look at myself. The burns on my left hand left the knuckle showing through, and for the first time I discovered that my left foot was wounded, blood was oozing out of the laceholes, and my right hand was pretty badly burned too. I decided to try my limbs and see if they would work — and thank goodness they did.

The oxygen mask was still covering my face but my hands were in too bad a state to remove it. I tried but I couldn't manage it. I found too that I had lost a trouser leg and the other was badly torn. My tunic was just like a lot of smouldering torn rags, so I wasn't looking very smart! Then after a bit more of this dangling down business I began to ache all over and my arms and legs began to hurt a lot. When I got lower it was apparent that I was in danger of coming down in the sea and I knew that I wouldn't stand an earthly if I did as I would have been unable to swim a stroke with my hands like that. I managed to float inland and noticed that I was heading straight for a high-tension cable, but fortunately floated over it towards a nice open field. When I was about 100 feet from the ground I saw a cyclist and heard him ring his bell. This surprised me and I realised that my descent had been in total silence. I bellowed at the cyclist but I don't think that he heard me.

Finally, I touched down in a field — and fell over. Fortunately, the day was very calm and my parachute floated down without taking me along the ground, as they sometimes do. I had a piece of good news almost immediately. One of the people who had come along and witnessed the combat said that they had seen the Messerschmitt dive straight into the sea — so it hadn't been such a bad day after all!

The above account has been taken verbatim from a recording made by James Nicolson in 1940 for a BBC nationwide broadcast, and depicts with awesome authenticity the encounter waged over Southampton, which promulgated the award of the nation's highest military decoration, the Victoria Cross, which transpired to be the only distinction of this order to be given to a pilot of Fighter Command during the Battle of Britain — and indeed the conflict of 1939-45.

Why was this unique — and controversial — honour bestowed on Nicolson alone?

Was there any other reason besides the act of supreme gallantry and devotion to duty of an already wounded and badly burned young pilot? Much speculation and uncorroborated material has been written since 1940 — some of this quite irresponsible and unresearched.

Official records from various sources indisputably confirm the motivation and build-up within the hierarchy of the Air Ministry which influenced this decision in those epic, fateful days of 1940, when Britain stood along against the unchecked might of the Luftwaffe.

The enigma surrounding this controversial issue is revealed in the proceeding pages.

CHAPTER 1

The Early Years

From quiet homes and first beginning
Out to the undiscovered ends
Hilaire Belloc (Dedicatory Ode)

James Brindley Eric Nicolson was born in Hampstead, London, on 29 April 1917, and was the elder son of Dorothea and Leslie Nicolson, of Scottish extraction. Charles Gavin was a younger brother with sisters Lesley Elizabeth and Jeanne Frances. Within the family circle James was known as 'Bill' but to his friends in the Royal Air Force it was always 'Nick'. Although given the name Eric after an uncle killed in the war of 1914-18 he for some reason, known only to himself, omitted to use it. His father was of independent financial means but a semi-invalid resulting from injuries sustained in the war. His hobby was car racing and is reputed to have competed against, and beaten, Sir Malcolm Campbell at Brooklands in his Hispano Suiza. His mother, Dorothea, cared for a well-knit family with the eye of a loving, if regulated presence. Strikingly handsome, she left no doubt where Nick had inherited his shock of thick, curly hair and good looks. He gave the soubriquet of 'Cupie' to his sister Jeanne as he thought she resembled a cupie doll, which were popular and fashionable in their childhood. The family tended to lead an itinerant lifestyle in the southern counties, possibly due to father's restless temperament. They finally settled at Shoreham-by-Sea.

Nick's early education was spent at Yardley Court Preparatory School, Tonbridge, and later as a day boy at Tonbridge School from September 1930 to July 1934. A contemporary pupil — later Registrar —was Mr T C Cobb who recalls: *'James had no particularly outstanding abilities but was not without success either, as a cricketer and long-distance runner. Being a day-boy he did not take part in extra-curricular activities.'*

Another ex-Tonbridge pupil, Mr B G Mabey, recalls his friendship with Nicolson: *'Cotton, Miller, Nicolson and I shared the same tutor, and we decided that he didn't really take sufficient interest in our tutorial. We decided to place a small bundle of paper, containing a firework, into his fireplace whilst he was reading his newspaper. Beforehand we had asked for a volunteer to throw the paper in — and Nicolson did this. In hindsight, this perhaps gives one some premonition of the bravery that he was to exhibit later in 'our finest hour' . After protestations following the event, the tutor issued a three letter word — 'out' —and we were duly admonished the following day by our Housemaster. I am pleased that an interest is being shown in Nicolson, as I have at times thought that perhaps his exploits were slightly overlooked. I later met him and he was at pains to tell me that the action for which he was awarded the Victoria Cross was not out of bravery but out of pure anger. I am delighted that his undoubted bravery is to be publicised as we owe so much to these valiant people who gave their lives for our freedom.'* Nick was an enthusiastic member of the Tonbridge School Officer Training Corps during his tenure there, attaining the rank of Corporal.

The call of the Colours

On leaving Tonbridge School with good all-round, but not distinctive grades, Nick was employed at Ricardo Engines (now Ricardo Consulting Engineers) as an experimental engineer, based at Shoreham-by-Sea. His younger brother, Gavin, was also employed by the company a year or so later . Nick's keen interest in aviation and the exploits of the 'aces' of World War I prompted him to seek other horizons and he volunteered for training in the Royal Air Force. He was granted a four-year Short Service Commission with the rank of Acting Pilot Officer (on probation) in the General Duties branch.

He commenced his training at the de Havilland School of Flying, White Waltham, where the aircraft on charge were the de Havilland DH82(a) Tiger Moth. His log book records that his training was entirely on aircraft G-ADIB, carrying out 'taxi-ing and handling of engine and action in case of fire, effect of controls, straight and level flying, stalling, climbing and gliding, landing and judging distances, spinning, climbing and gliding turns'. On 14 November he went solo after eleven hours flying dual with his instructor 'Carrol', eventually passing out on 16 November 1936 under the Chief Instructor Captain Reeves. Further training followed: 'advanced forced landings, sideslipping, instrument flying, aerobatics', After 24 hours solo his proficiency rating was 'average — no special faults'.

No 10 Flying Training School, Ternhill

After a short spell of leave he was posted to No 10 Flying Training School flying Hawker Hart and Audax biplanes, going solo in Hart T.5019 on 19 January 1937. It is interesting to note that on the flying staff were two officers who were to be associated with his future service. Nick's Flight Commander at Ternhill was Flight Lieutenant E W Whitley, an Australian, who was later to become Group Captain E W Whitley DSO DFC, Station Commander at Royal Air Force Church Fenton, in 1945. The other officer was the charismatic Earl of Bandon. Known as 'Paddy' Bandon, he was a very popular officer with a great sense of humour, he went on to achieve a distinguished career as Air Officer Commanding 221 Group in the Burma campaign in 1944 and later held the rank of Air Chief Marshal when in command of the Allied Air Forces —Central Europe in 1963. It reflects his tremendous sense of humour to relate that he must have been the only C-in-C to have opened a swimming pool by diving into it in full dress after carefully handing in his hat to his

Aide. Behind his desk at NATO headquarters he had the notice saying "*Work fascinates me — I can sit and look at it for hours*". At 59 years of age he must have been the oldest serving pilot in any Air Force. He retired in 1963 after 40 years service.

Nick had accumulated 150 hours flying time (1 July 1937) and had passed all his tests successfully with a rating of 'average'. He was then posted to No 3 Armament Training Corps at Sutton Bridge in Lincolnshire for specialised training in gunnery. This course included Vickers ground grouping, Vickers quarter practice, Vickers astern practice, and Vickers beam practice. On 20 July the five Hart trainees returned to Ternhill following a satisfactory assessment by Flt Lt Cattell, OC 'C' Flight.

James Brindley Nicolson VC DFC RAF

A young schoolboy

James with mother

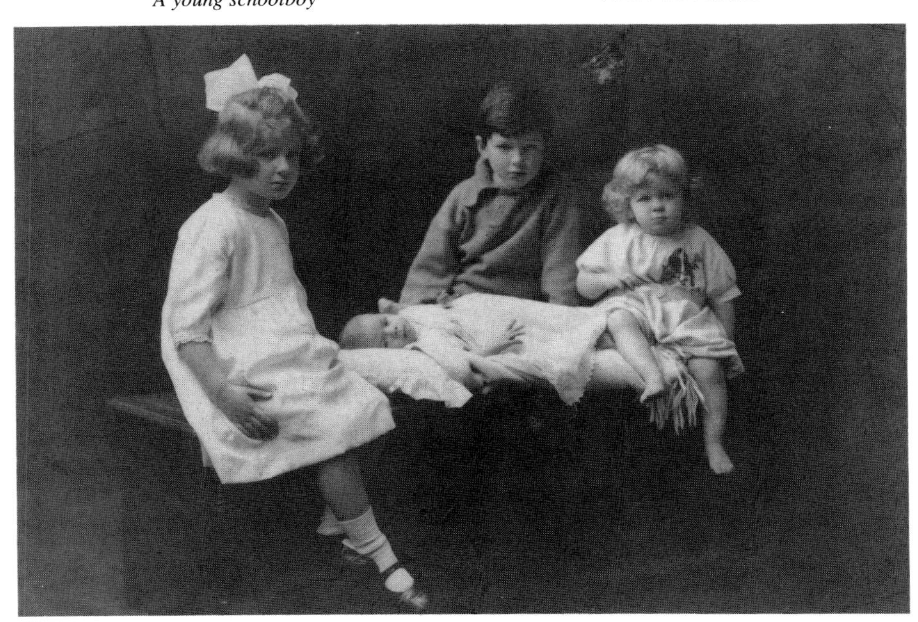
A young Nick with brother and sisters

Headquarters and Instructional Staff *Source: RAF Museum, Hendon.*
No 10 Flying Training School —Ternhill 1936
Standing (left to right): C. J. Moule, F/Lt Vintras, F/O Savill, F/Lt Rigby, F/O Read, F/O Chambers, D. R. Orchard, E. Johnston, F/O Whitley, F/O Pilling, F/O Nicholl, F/O Thompson.
Sitting (left to right): F/Lt Eayrs, S/L Walker, W/C Foreman, G/C Darley, S/L Bowen-Buscarlet, F/Lt Earl of Bandon, F/Lt Gray.

Line up of Avro Tutor trainers.

The Earl of Bandon, No 10 FTS

Hawker Demons warming up.

Nick and cricket team, Ricardo Engineers, 1936

CHAPTER 2

Life and romance at Church Fenton

'Turn you where your lady is
. . . and claim her with a loving kiss'
The Merchant of Venice (Act III)

Nick thoroughly enjoyed his time at No 10 Flying Training School, now a successfully encountered hurdle in his early flying career, the next challenge being his posting to No 72(F) Squadron, based at Royal Air Force Church Fenton, in North Yorkshire, adjacent to the village of that name. This was a region steeped in military history dating back to the Roman conquest, and where, in 1461, 30,000 soldiers were killed in one day by close hand-to-hand fighting at nearby Towton Moor. This was one of the fiercest confrontations of the War of the Roses when 'the waters of Cockbeck (local stream) ran red with blood'. With this bellicose backcloth and amid local protestations against the use of prime agricultural farmland, Royal Air Force Church Fenton's long and distinguished military role was established. The station was to form an important part of the Ministry of Defence 'expansion programme' and central to many new Bomber Command stations projected for Yorkshire and Lincolnshire. It was officially opened on 1 April 1937 under the aegis of the Air Officer Commanding No 11 Group, Fighter Command. The station as planned under the original contract was scheduled for completion in 1939 but in 1937 was only partially completed. However, the infrastructure was sufficient to provide the essential facilities and afford operational status, ie — the barrack blocks, NAAFI canteen, mess decks, guardroom, sick bay and hangars were complete, but had only grass runways, which was to create problems in wet weather for the narrow-tracked, nose-heavy Spitfires later.

Nick reported for duty on 7 August 1937 full of enthusiasm and expectancy. At this time there were two resident fighter squadrons on the station. No 213 equipped with Gloster Gauntlett biplane fighters, and No 72(F) Squadron flying Gloster Gladiators. The Gauntlett was the worthy forerunner of the more advanced Gladiator, which was the latest and fastest four-gun fighter and destined to be the last of the biplane types. It was highly manoeuvrable and aerobatic, and popular with both pilots and groundcrew. No 72 had recently arrived from Tangmere where it had been reformed on 22 February 1937, following disbandment after the world war of 1914, where it had fought with distinction, emerging from the conflict with a first-class reputation.

The Commander at this time was Squadron Leader E J L Hope who had been a member of the recently successful British Schneider Trophy racing team. Nick's log book records that on 9 August he made his first introductory flight in the 'new type' — Gladiator K.6130 — for a duration of 35 minutes. He obviously revelled in the new aircraft, soon becoming expert in the handling of the type and quickly developing an affinity for it. Training included slow flying, landings, local map reading and cross country exercises, sighting practice on ground targets, formation practice and night flying, for the most part using Gladiator K.6130. He developed into a first class pilot and aerial marksman, regularly taking part in flying displays and flypasts. His tenacity, confidence and enthusiasm quickly earned him the reputation of the 'press-on type'. Socially a fun-loving extrovert, gregarious and born mimic he could be relied on to be at the forefront of any activities, and although not a rugby player was always in the mêlée of after-mess frolics. Possessed of a good musical ear and memory, he later put this gift to good use with his above average knowledge of swing and jazz. Conversely, he could on occasion be stubborn and obstreperous with a mild disregard for accepted military convention and protocol —something of a maverick ! He integrated well into the squadron and was popular with both his fellow officers and ground staff, who came to know him as 'the boy' because of his youthful looks and tall (6ft 3½in), loose-limbed frame. He regularly gave his 'A' Flight technicians a packet of Players for presenting, normally on a Friday, a clean and tidily prepared aircraft. It was not an uncommon sight in off-duty hours to see Nick and his fellow officers cavorting around the hangar walking on their hands. Also, off-limit car racing — in reverse — was sometimes high-spiritedly indulged in.

Nick's first Flight Commander was Flight Lieutenant F W (Hiram) Smith, a Canadian, whose acquaintanceship developed into a long and enduring friendship. As his mentor, an assessment of Nick was *'a very good pilot and excellent front gun shot'. A good friend — I greatly enjoyed his company. Later, after the war started in 1939 and we were stationed at Drem, on the Firth of Forth, he illustrated his determination and a streak of stubbornness. We were required to do long periods on duty, day and night, as there was a great shortage of operational pilots. No 72 Squadron was the only regular squadron between Catterick and Wick, and the two Auxiliary Squadrons — Nos 602 and 603 — were in the process of re-equipping with Spitfires and weren't fully operational. Nick had flu and should have been in bed but insisted in doing his full period on duty, huddled in a full leather Irvin suit by the stove in the Flight hut. He refused to go off duty, but luckily no order came to 'scramble'. Had we been ordered off I would have had to restrain him from taking off as he really wasn't fit enough to fly.'*

On 12 October 1937 he was confirmed in appointment and graded as a Pilot Officer, which gave rise to much celebration and jollifications in the mess. It was about this time when attending a dance at the Riley-Smith Hall, Tadcaster, not far from the base, that he met Muriel Kendal, the attractive daughter of a local farmer located at the old-world village of Kirkby Wharfe, some two miles from the station.

There was a great mutual attraction, and it was not long before he proposed to her, but she refused, saying *'I'm older than you, and my parents don't approve'*. However, Nick had made up his mind that Muriel was the girl for him, and with characteristic persistence and tenacity for over a year, she relented. They became engaged in January 1938, which was duly announced at the Conservative Ball in Tadcaster.

1938 was to be the only peacetime year of operational training for the two resident squadrons prior to the outbreak of WW2, and was to prove of interest and incident. Early in the year, 213 Squadron left for Wittering, to be replaced by No 64 led by Squadron Leader Victor Beamish, performing formation flying over the area in their Demon I aircraft on the day of their arrival. Major personnel changes took place, Wing Commander G T Richardson succeeding Wing Commander W E Swann as Station Commander, and the command of 72 Squadron changing from Squadron Leader Hope to Squadron Leader B H Rodgers and subsequently Squadron Leader R R Lees, an Australian.

In common with other squadrons under training and taking on charge new aircraft and aircrew, 72 was no exception to the initial technical 'gremlins' and training mishaps. Gun synchronisation problems due to interrupter gear malfunction delayed the air-to-air and air-to-ground firing programme. The two-bladed wooden Watts airscrew were being holed near the blade root ends by the inner (fuselage) guns. Eventually the air firing exercises were completed by using the mainplane guns only. The first squadron casualty occurred when Gladiator K.6131 was lost near Barnsley. The pilot had to abandon his aircraft during an induced flat spin. He left it late to bale out but landed safely. The squadron was less fortunate in a later mishap in July, when the pilot was killed in an air collision whilst taking part in a camera-gun exercise as part of fighter tactics.

On 20 May the two resident squadrons combined to give an exhilarating air display to 3000 visitors who braved the rain — the first Open Day at Church Fenton. Home defence exercises took place in early August, 64 Squadron was detached to Digby and No 72 to Wittering. During these exercises four aircraft of 64 Squadron were lost in unusual circumstances. On the night of 7 August following the take-off of four Demons, a dense fog descended obscuring a wide area of England. The aircraft flew southwards in an attempt to find clearer conditions before running out of petrol. The effort however was abortive, and with petrol supplies almost exhausted, an order was received from the Sector Commander at Duxford to fly on a course of 225 degrees magnetic — and abandon aircraft. The crew of the four aircraft subsequently baled out safely, the four pilotless aircraft flew on into the foggy night.

The station took on an added air of efficiency and 'spit and polish' for the impending visit of Air Marshal, Sir Hugh Dowding, Air Officer Commanding Fighter Command — the occasion being the Presentation of the Squadron Crest — and Reunion.

On 29 June the second fatal accident occurred during a detail of formation flying. Two Gladiators touched during a manoeuvre, Gladiators K.6138 and K.6139 being the aircraft involved. Flight Lieutenant W F Pharazyn was killed when K.6139 crashed, the pilot of the other aircraft managed to get down in damaged condition. The accident had a sobering effect on the squadron personnel, many of whom had never before seen an aircraft crash with fatal result. Flight Lieutenant Pharazyn was of Swiss extraction.

Shortly after this, an incident occurred which could have resulted in an accident, but fate was kind that day to Pilot Officer Henstock, the pilot of Gladiator K.6141. He was taking part with another aircraft on a map-reading exercise over the North Yorkshire moors when his aircraft developed engine trouble. He made base as the engine oil pressure started to fluctuate and slowly drop, black smoke belching from the exhaust and distinctly noisy. An examination of the engine disclosed a considerable amount of metal chippings in the oil pressure filter.

Without doubt, 1939 was the most progressive and meaningful in the standards of training and new aircraft at Church Fenton, No 72 taking on charge a batch of new Spitfires — an aircraft to distinguish itself as a fighter above all others in the ensuing momentous years to come against the increasingly belligerent Nazi Germany. Both 64 and 72 Squadrons participated in the air displays given in May to celebrate Empire Air Day, all the exercises performed being of special significance in respect to training, including a massed flight of six squadrons over the Midlands. Following the earlier Munich crisis, and acting on orders from No 12 Group Headquarters, all aircraft on the station were armed and brought to 'immediate war readiness'. Pilot Officer Desmond Sheen, an Australian, and later Group Captain, remembers the occasion well: *'In consideration to Empire Air Day, although we were converted to Spitfires we kept behind a couple of Gladiators. Although I was not in the same flight as Nick, we were teamed up to do synchronised aerobatics. Oddly enough, these were permitted, but formation aerobatics were not. This silly ruling was, much later, reversed! However, just before we were due to take off for the display a crack was detected in the wing spar of Nick's aircraft, and regrettably, we had to cancel. In the event, we had not altogether finished with the services of the Gladiators, as, when we later moved to Acklington in March 1940, the airfield was waterlogged and taxi-ing with Spitfires could only be done with someone sitting on the tail. The Gladiator, with its cantilever undercarriage and Dowty internally sprung wheels could cope with these 'minor lakes', but the Spitfire needed great care, with its narrow track undercarriage and small wheels — and great weight of Merlin engine. We reactivated some Gladiators particularly for night/early morning convoy patrols. Nick and I were good friends, and one way and another we had a lot of good times together.'*

In July 1939, Muriel and Nick were married at St John's Church, Kirkby Wharfe, the ceremony being attended by close relatives and friends, and a contingent of Nick's fellow officers from Church Fenton.

Aircraftsman-2 Ralph Nugent recalls his introduction to 72 Squadron in April 1939: *'Coming from a unit of 'spit and polish' — No 11 FTS Shawbury — where every church parade had two or three bands and about 3000 men on parade it was a luxury to arrive at the squadron discip office to be welcomed by the Adjutant, Flying Officer T A F Elsdon, and passed to the Commanding Officer, Squadron*

Leader R R Lees for a word of welcome. I was taken to 'A' Flight office where I met Sgt. Eagle, NCO in charge, then taken next door to meet Officer i/c Flight, Flight Lieutenant F M Smith. I was somewhat overwhelmed, as the office was full of pilots, standing around the wall, sitting on the window-ledge, and sprawling in chairs. All seemed genuinely interested in the AC-2 being introduced to them individually. The first was dressed in a blue Australian uniform, FO D F B Sheen (Desmond), PO St Pigg (Ossie), FO J B Nicolson (Nick), PO J W Villa (Pancho), PO N C H Robson, PO R J Walker, FO L F Henstock, PO E J Wilcox, Sgt B Douthwaite (Dizzy), Sgt Steere (he turned down a commission several times) and Sgts Staples, Hamlyn, Norfolk and Pocock. They were mainly about 19-22 years of age, and many did not live another year. The squadron had just taken on charge 18 Spitfires and were busy converting Gladiators for desert service.

I sat on the tail of Nick's aircraft many times, being subjected to hurricane force winds whilst he checked his mags. As a member of the station dance band I remember playing at a garden fete in one of the big houses in the locality. Looking down from the band's elevated position some five feet above the lower garden and roadway, Pancho and Nick, sporting a red Series 'E' MG loaded a 24-bottle case of beer into the back of the car, about to drive off to another party. We waved 'good-luck' and laughed at the situation! Being in the station band I played many times in the Officers Mess, and remember Muriel's arrival. It is difficult to identify with those stirring times — it now seems to be another country. Squadron and station life were never to revert! I can recall clearly Nick giving a solo display in a Gladiator at the Air Show on Empire Air Day, the aerobatics which were mainly centred above Flying Control at about 300-500 feet enthralling the crowd, especially as he was doing a running commentary. For me, that last peacetime summer for six years, stands out for all time. When war was declared on 3 September 1939, we were instructed to move the aircraft to a safer parking area, at the edge of the airfield nearest the village. An Army detachment guarded the road and a password was required to pass through the gate. Blast-bays ran the full length of the road and security was intensified as 'spies' were reported to be active. NCOs and 'erks' were given the unpopular task of guard duty to perform and allocated a rifle, bayonet and five rounds of ammunition. We stalked the Duty Officer — Nick, Pancho or Ossie when they carried out their rounds, and tried to scare them with our challenges. We departed Church Fenton for Leconfield by road, only to be posted on 28 October to Drem in Scotland, the ground crews being flown by aircraft of Imperial Airways — the Hannibal, Ensign and Elsinore. One morning Red Section was detailed to carry out early morning patrols, and standing in front of the Flight Office I watched Nick and Ossie supporting Pancho as they hurried to their aircraft, Pancho's flying boots dragging in the frosty grass as they went, their 'chutes bouncing on their legs. The take-off was spectacular as they went down the hill. As equipment assistant, I had found a way of exchanging the pilot's silk inner liners for their flying gloves, and supplied everyone up with new ones, but for some reason overlooked Nick. Some time later I was congratulating two newly-commissioned Sgt Pilots when Nick approached me and asked why he had not been issued with a pair of new liners, as the others had been? He was most hurt and I quickly replied that the omission would be corrected. Unfortunately, I was unable to live up to my good intentions as we had run out of stock, much to my chagrin. I regret to this day that this happened. In retrospect, those epic days with 72 Squadron were the best days of my life.'

The wager

During their time together with No 72 Squadron, the friendship between Nick and his Flight Commander, Flt Lt Hiram Smith flourished. They were busy by day and night chasing the elusive Do.17 and He. 111 reconnaissance aircraft that came across the North Sea. The topic arose as to the first one to shoot down an enemy aircraft. They had a bet who would be the first one to have the honour, the stake being a princely £1.00 on the outcome. However, they were soon to go their different ways when Nick was transferred to the newly formed No 249. Hiram shared the destruction of a Do. 17 on 29 June 1940 with two other pilots of 72 Squadron, when they intercepted a raid of 100 plus enemy aircraft as they approached the Northumberland coast. The formation comprised a main bomber force of He. 111's with an escort of Bf. 110 fighters operating from bases in Norway. It proved to be an expensive operation for them. Hiram attacked three He.111's in succession, two of which streamed smoke from their engines and one blew up in a huge ball of fire. He directed his remaining ammunition at a Bf.110 and thereby established a lead on Nick, but he didn't know it at the time. It was to be the end of September before they met again — under a much different set of circumstances.

No 72 Squadron at Church Fenton 1938

Presenting the Colour to No 72 Squadron by Lord Dowding, 1938

Royal Air Force Station, Church Fenton
EMPIRE AIR DAY —Sat., 20 May, 1939

FLYING PROGRAMME —Part 1

Event No.	*Time*	*Event*
1	*14.00*	***Take-off by Wing of 18 Aircraft*** *The formation consists of 9 Blenheim aircraft of No. 64 (Fighter) Squadron and 9 Spitfire aircraft of No. 72 (Fighter) Squadron. After taking off these aircraft will form up into Wing formation (Squadrons line astern) and will turn over the Aerodrome at 14-21 hours.* *NOTE: The Blenheim although originally designed as a Bomber is now, owing to its speed and manoeuverability, also being used as a two seater fighter.*
2	*14.08*	***Individual Acrobatics--Gladiator Aircraft*** *The aircraft used in this event is a Gloster Gladiator single-seater fighter (Bristol Mercury Engine). The aerobatics performed will include loops, rolls, upward rolls and rocket loops.*
	14.10	*Visit of the Secretary of State for Air.* *Arrival by air of the Secretary of State for Air, the Rt. Hon. Sir Kingsley Wood, and Chief of the Air Staff, Air Chief Marshal Sir Cyril Newall, GCB, CMG CBE AM*
3	*14.25*	***Demonstration of Speed by Spitfire Aircraft.*** *Three Spitfire aircraft will dive over the aerodrome to demonstrate the speed at which modern fighter aircraft now travel. Afterwards No. 72 (F) Squadron will land by Sections of three aircraft.*
4	*14.35*	***Air Drill by 4 Blenheim Aircraft of No. 64 (F) Squadron.*** *All the aircraft in this formation are fitted with wireless and orders will be transmitted from the ground to the pilots in the air. The aircraft will be seen to be changing formation.*
5	*14.55*	***Synchronised Aerobatics--Gladiator Aircraft.*** *Two Gladiator aircraft of No. 72 (F) Squadron will carry out aerobatics together. This event calls for very careful timing and the orders given by one pilot to the other will be broadcast over the loud speaker.*

6	***15.15***	***Air Race.*** *This will be a handicap race for different types of aircraft, the top speeds of which vary between 360mph and 120mph.* *The following types will take part in this event: Spitfire, Blenheim, Gladiator, Battle, Demon, Hind, Magister and Tutor.* *The race will be flown over a triangular course, the aerodrome being one of the turning points.*
7	***16.03***	***Fly Past by Formation of Battle Aircraft*** *These aircraft will arrive from another R.A.F. Station and will fly over the Aerodrome in formation. The Battle is a medium bomber type.*
8	***16.10***	***Aerobatics by Tutor Aircraft.*** *The Tutor is a training aircraft fitted with an Armstrong Siddeley engine of 220 h.p.*
9	***16.20***	***Demonstration by Lysander Aircraft.*** *The Lysander is used by Army Co-operation Units and has the characteristics of quick take-off, slow landing speed and good control at slow flying speeds. This obtained with the help of slots and flaps fitted to the wings.*
10	***16.45***	***Quick getaway by 3 Spitfire Aircraft.*** *This event represents the normal work of a Fighter Squadron in carrying out the interception of hostile bombers. On a given signal the pilots run to their aircraft, start the engines and take-off with the least possible delay. Once in the air, orders can be passed to the Fighters by radio-telephony.*
11	***17.00***	***Attack by 3 fighters v. 1 Bomber.*** *One Blenheim of No. 64 (F) Squadron, representing a Bomber, will be attacked by 3 Spitfires of No. 72 (Fighter) Squadron.*
12	***17.15***	***Fly Past of Aircraft in Park.***

Nicolson in his Gladiator (photo taken by his Flight Commander 'Hiram' Smith)

Daily inspection of Gladiators of 72 Squadron.

Nicolson's much used 6140.

No 72 Squadron at Church Fenton, 1938. Left to right: F/Lt. F. M. Smith (Canadian), F/O J. B. Nicolson, F/O J. B. W. Humpherson (later killed), F/O D. F. B. Sheen DFC (Australian), F/O O. St. John Pigg (later killed), F/O R. A. Thompson (New Zealand), F/O T. A. F. Elsdon OBE DFC.

Gladiators over Church Fenton No 72 Squadron, 1938

Crew of Gladiator 6141.

Spitfires in formation (No 72 Squadron), Church Fenton, 1939

The beautiful bride (1939).

The Nicolson wedding at Kirkby Wharfe

(1207–117) Wt. 25812—1600 17,500 10/38 I.S. 700 **FORM 414 (A)**

SUMMARY of FLYING and ASSESSMENTS FOR YEAR COMMENCING 1st ..... JUNE *1938

[* For Officer, insert "JUNE"; For Airman Pilot, insert "AUGUST."]

	S.E. AIRCRAFT		M.E. AIRCRAFT		TOTAL	GRAND TOTAL All Service Flying
	Day	Night	Day	Night		
DUAL	·20	/	1·45	/	2·05	54·10
PILOT	222·10	21·35	/	/	243·45.	509·25.
PASSENGER	—	—	—	—	/	2·50.

ASSESSMENT of ABILITY

(To be assessed as :—Exceptional, Above the Average, Average, or Below the Average)

(i) AS A ..... F. ..... † PILOT ..... Above Average.

(ii) AS PILOT–NAVIGATOR/NAVIGATOR ..... average.

(iii) IN BOMBING ..... —

(iv) IN AIR GUNNERY ..... Above Average

† Insert :—"F.", "L.B.", "G.R." "F.B." etc.

ANY POINTS IN FLYING OR AIRMANSHIP WHICH SHOULD BE WATCHED.

.....

.....

Date ..... 14. 6. 39.

Signature ..... [signature] S/Ldr

Officer Commanding ..... No 72 Sqdn.

Nick's Flying Assessment with No 72 Squadron, June 1938

A "Sunday Dispatch" Page To Help Everyone Defend The Country

THE War Office has issued these diagram pictures of enemy troop-carrying 'planes. They are intended to guide Local Defence Volunteers and all members of the public.

Some of these pictures have been published elsewhere in the past few days, but this page contains many more details and also silhouettes of comparable British bombers. It is the only complete chart. Cut it out and hang it on your wall.

If you see an aeroplane that resembles an enemy, tell the police, an air raid warden, or the L.D.V. at once.

Here are some simple points to remember:

If the 'plane has more than two engines it is probably a German.

The 3-engined Junkers Ju 52 has one engine in the nose, looking like the head of a fly. These have been the 'planes most used for parachutists.

The Junkers Ju 90 has wings that sweep backwards like a swallow in flight.

Note the square-cut edges of the wings and tails of the Junkers 'planes.

If a bomber is flying low in daylight, note the colour.

British bombers are mostly painted black on the underside. (There are some silver or light green.)

The badge painted on British 'planes is like a red, white, and blue target, with the red as the bull's-eye.

German bombers are painted light blue-grey under the fuselage and wings.

Their badge is a black cross, outlined with a white band. The white band itself is outlined in black.

A black swastika is usually carried on the tail of the 'plane.

THESE ARE THE TYPES OF GERMAN AIRCRAFT YOU ARE MOST LIKELY TO SEE

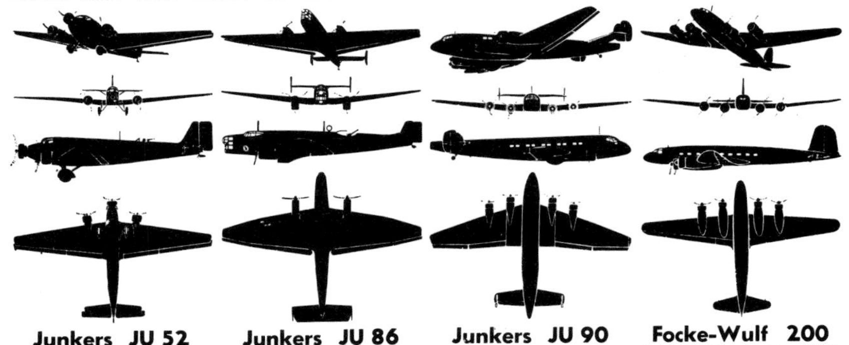

Junkers JU 52

The Junkers 52 is the most important troop carrier and the one normally used by the Germans for parachute troops. It has a wing span of 96 feet and a length of 62 feet. Its distinctive features are:

1. Three engines.
2. Low wing.
3. Single square-cut rudder.
4. Sharply tapered wings.
5. Square-cut wing tips and tail plane.
6. Fixed undercarriage.

Junkers JU 86

Distinctive features of the Junkers 86, which has a wing span of 73ft. 8in. and a length of 57ft. 4in., are:

1. Two engines.
2. Low wing.
3. Two square-cut rudders.
4. Sharply tapered wings.
5. Square-cut wing tips and tail plane.
6. Retractable undercarriage.

Junkers JU 90

The Junkers Ju 90, the biggest of the Junkers bombers, has a wing span of 115ft. and is 86ft. long. Its distinctive features are:

1. Four engines.
2. Low wing.
3. Two rudders.
4. Tapered wings.
5. Leading edge of wing has very pronounced "sweep back."
6. Square-cut wing tips and tail plane.
7. Retractable undercarriage.

Focke-Wulf 200

The Focke-Wulf 200 Condor has a wing span of 108 feet and is 78 feet long. Its principal features are:

1. Four engines.
2. Low wing.
3. Single rudder.
4. Tapered wing.
5. Rounded wing tips and tail plane.
6. Retractable undercarriage.
7. Smooth stream-lined fuselage.

BUT DON'T MISTAKE THEM FOR THESE BRITISH BOMBERS

Whitley IV

Twin-engined long-range bomber. Undercarriage retracts. Rectangular fuselage, slightly tapered wings. Twin fins and rudders. Wing span, 84ft. 0in.; length, 69ft. 3in.

Hampden

Twin-engined Handley Page Hampden long-range bomber. Undercarriage retracts. Deep, narrow, rectangular fuselage with rounded transparent nose. Twin fins and rudders. Highly tapered wings. Wing span 69ft. 2in.; length, 53ft. 7in.

Lockheed Hudson B-14

Twin-engined bomber. Undercarriage retracts. Deep, short fuselage with twin fins and rudders and cantilever tailplane. Highly tapered wings with pointed tips. Wing span, 65ft. 6in.; length, 44ft. 2½in.

Cut Out This "Sunday Dispatch" Page And Pin It On The Wall At Home Or At Your Office

Blenheim

Twin-engined Bristol Blenheim Mk. I long-range fighter and high-speed bomber. Retracting undercarriage. Fixed tail wheel. Short transparent nose, straight tapered wings with pointed tips, deep motor nacelles, bisected by wings. Single fin and rudder. Wing span 56ft. 4in.; length 39ft. 9in.

Wellington

Twin-engined Wellington Mk. Ia long-range bomber. Power-operated turret in nose with two guns. Similar turret in tail. Undercarriage retracts backwards. Deep, well-streamlined fuselage. Highly tapered wings. Tall single fin and rudder and cantilever tailplane. Wing span, 86ft. 1in.; length, 61ft. 3in.

MEMORISE THIS

Engines three or engines four?
There's a Nazi at the door!

* * *

If the fly's head comes in view
Maybe paratroopers too.

* * *

If the wings as swallow's lie
"Still a Nazi" is the cry.

* * *

And among the other things
Nazis like the square-clipped wings.

* * *

Britain's 'planes have underpart
Black as any Nazi heart.

Harrogate INVITES YOU TO TAKE A CURE & HOLIDAY at the NATION'S SPA
Write for particulars of the "All-inclusive Cure" Scheme. Holiday Guide and Hotel Accommodation to L. Wilshere, Information Bureau, HARROGATE
TRAVEL BY RAIL
MONTHLY RETURN TICKETS Any Train. Any Day. From All Parts.

GRAVES Beats the World For Quality & Value

KAYSER-BONDOR
Price for 32-36 inch size was quoted in this newspaper last Sunday at 8 11. This was an error and should have read 7.11.

HOW TO SPOT PARATROOPS

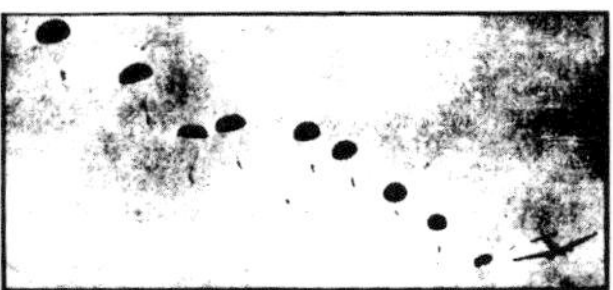

Note that paratroops drop in close formation and in larger numbers than the ordinary crew of an aeroplane. Over their uniforms they wear grey gabardine overalls. The front has a zip fastener.

Troop-dropping parachutes—this is one—are larger than normal. There is no "pilot" parachute, and the canopy is scalloped. They can drop from 300 feet.

FULL PROGRAMME OF ENTERTAINMENTS
AMPLE ACCOMMODATION
SOUTHPORT
TRAVEL BY RAIL • MONTHLY RETURN TICKETS
Official Guide Post free from S.D. Wolstenholme, Town Hall, Southport

The equipment carried by parachute troops.

The modern household soap
IS WHITE!
For washing, scrubbing, cleaning right
For making clothes and dishes bright
For keeping your expenses light—
Use Sylvan Soap—the soap that's white!
SYLVAN SOAP 2½D
use SYLVAN and SAVE
THOMAS HEDLEY & CO. LIMITED, NEWCASTLE-ON-TYNE AND MANCHESTER

Issued by the Ministry of Information  *in co-operation with the War Office and the Ministry of Home Security.*

If the INVADER comes

WHAT TO DO — AND HOW TO DO IT

THE Germans threaten to invade Great Britain. If they do so they will be driven out by our Navy, our Army and our Air Force. Yet the ordinary men and women of the civilian population will also have their part to play. Hitler's invasions of Poland, Holland and Belgium were greatly helped by the fact that the civilian population was taken by surprise. They did not know what to do when the moment came. *You must not be taken by surprise.* This leaflet tells you what general line you should take. More [de]tailed instructions will be given you when the danger comes nearer. Meanwhile, read these instructions carefully and be prepared to carry them out.

I

When Holland and Belgium were invaded, the civilian population fled from their homes. They crowded on the roads, in cars, in carts, on bicycles and on foot, and so helped the enemy by preventing their own armies from advancing against the invaders. You must not allow that to happen here. Your first rule, therefore, is :—

(1) IF THE GERMANS COME, BY PARACHUTE, AEROPLANE OR SHIP, YOU MUST REMAIN WHERE YOU ARE. THE ORDER IS "STAY PUT".

If the Commander in Chief decides that the place where you live must be evacuated, he will tell you when and how to leave. Until you receive such orders you must remain where you are. If you run away, you will be exposed to far greater danger because you will be machine-gunned from the air as were civilians in Holland and Belgium, and you will also block the roads by which our own armies will advance to turn the Germans out.

II

There is another method which the Germans adopt in their invasion. They make use of the civilian population in order to create confusion and panic. They spread false rumours and issue false instructions. In order to prevent this, you should obey the second rule, which is as follows :—

(2) DO NOT BELIEVE RUMOURS AND DO NOT SPREAD THEM. WHEN YOU RECEIVE AN ORDER, MAKE QUITE SURE THAT IT IS A TRUE ORDER AND NOT A FAKED ORDER. MOST OF YOU KNOW YOUR POLICEMEN AND YOUR A.R.P. WARDENS BY SIGHT, YOU CAN TRUST THEM. IF YOU KEEP YOUR HEADS, YOU CAN ALSO TELL WHETHER A MILITARY OFFICER IS REALLY BRITISH OR ONLY PRETENDING TO BE SO. IF IN DOUBT ASK THE POLICEMAN OR THE A.R.P. WARDEN. USE YOUR COMMON SENSE.

Source: H.M.S.O.

Britain on Guard

III

The Army, the Air Force and the Local Defence Volunteers cannot be everywhere at once. The ordinary man and woman must be on the watch. If you see anything suspicious, do not rush round telling your neighbours all about it. Go at once to the nearest policeman, police-station, or military officer and tell them exactly what you saw. Train yourself to notice the exact time and place where you saw anything suspicious, and try to give exact information. Try to check your facts. The sort of report which a military or police officer wants from you is something like this :—

> "At 5.30 p.m. to-night I saw twenty cyclists come into Little Squashborough from the direction of Great Mudtown. They carried some sort of automatic rifle or gun. I did not see anything like artillery. They were in grey uniforms."

Be calm, quick and exact. The third rule, therefore, is as follows :—

(3) KEEP WATCH. IF YOU SEE ANYTHING SUSPICIOUS, NOTE IT CAREFULLY AND GO AT ONCE TO THE NEAREST POLICE OFFICER OR STATION, OR TO THE NEAREST MILITARY OFFICER. DO NOT RUSH ABOUT SPREADING VAGUE RUMOURS. GO QUICKLY TO THE NEAREST AUTHORITY AND GIVE HIM THE FACTS.

IV

Remember that if parachutists come down near your home, they will not be feeling at all brave. They will not know where they are, they will have no food, they will not know where their companions are. They will want you to give them food, means of transport and maps. They will want you to tell them where they have landed, where their comrades are, and where our own soldiers are. The fourth rule, therefore, is as follows :—

(4) DO NOT GIVE ANY GERMAN ANYTHING. DO NOT TELL HIM ANYTHING. HIDE YOUR FOOD AND YOUR BICYCLES. HIDE YOUR MAPS. SEE THAT THE ENEMY GETS NO PETROL. IF YOU HAVE A CAR OR MOTOR BICYCLE, PUT IT OUT OF ACTION WHEN NOT IN USE. IT IS NOT ENOUGH TO REMOVE THE IGNITION KEY; YOU MUST MAKE IT USELESS TO ANYONE EXCEPT YOURSELF.

IF YOU ARE A GARAGE PROPRIETOR, YOU MUST WORK OUT A PLAN TO PROTECT YOUR STOCK OF PETROL AND YOUR CUSTOMERS' CARS. REMEMBER THAT TRANSPORT AND PETROL WILL BE THE INVADER'S MAIN DIFFICULTIES. MAKE SURE THAT NO INVADER WILL BE ABLE TO GET HOLD OF YOUR CARS, PETROL, MAPS OR BICYCLES.

V

You may be asked by Army and Air Force officers to help in many ways. For instance, the time may come when you will receive orders to block roads or streets in order to prevent the enemy from advancing. Never block a road unless you are told which one you must block. Then you can help by felling trees, wiring them together or blocking the roads with cars. Here, therefore, is the fifth rule :—

(5) BE READY TO HELP THE MILITARY IN ANY WAY. BUT DO NOT BLOCK ROADS UNTIL ORDERED TO DO SO BY THE MILITARY OR L.D.V. AUTHORITIES.

VI

If you are in charge of a factory, store or other works, organise its defence at once. If you are a worker, make sure that you understand the system of defence that has been organised and know what part you have to play in it. Remember always that parachutists and fifth column men are powerless against any organised resistance. They can only succeed if they can create disorganisation. Make certain that no suspicious strangers enter your premises.

You must know in advance who is to take command, who is to be second in command, and how orders are to be transmitted. This chain of command must be built up and you will probably find that ex-officers or N.C.O.'s, who have been in emergencies before, are the best people to undertake such command. The sixth rule is therefore as follows :—

(6) IN FACTORIES AND SHOPS, ALL MANAGERS AND WORKMEN SHOULD ORGANISE SOME SYSTEM NOW BY WHICH A SUDDEN ATTACK CAN BE RESISTED.

VII

The six rules which you have now read give you a general idea of what to do in the event of invasion. More detailed instructions may, when the time comes, be given you by the Military and Police Authorities and by the Local Defence Volunteers; they will NOT be given over the wireless as that might convey information to the enemy. These instructions must be obeyed at once.

Remember always that the best defence of Great Britain is the courage of her men and women. Here is your seventh rule :—

(7) THINK BEFORE YOU ACT. BUT THINK ALWAYS OF YOUR COUNTRY BEFORE YOU THINK OF YOURSELF.

(52194) Wt. / 14,300,000 6/40 Bw.

Source: H.M.S.O.

Britain on Guard

To the Workers of Britain

YOU are one of Hitler's biggest stumbling-blocks. So long as you keep Britain's factories, mines, shipyards and other industries going at full blast, Hitler can't win—*and he knows it!*

That's why he will try all kinds of tricks to disorganize your work.

In France many factories and offices stopped work because of false rumours of parachute landings. Traitors telephoned false evacuation orders to workshops. In this way the industries of France were thrown out of gear and Hitler's victory was made secure.

This mustn't happen in *our* workshops! Every one of us must stay on the job in spite of air raids, rumours or parachutists, just as our soldiers have to—unless we get orders to evacuate from the police, the military or the Home Guard.

Remember, this is a People's War. Even though you may not wear a uniform, you will help Britain to win by carrying on at your desk or bench, no matter what happens.

. . . that's why you must **STAY PUT**

Issued by the Ministry of Information
Space presented to the nation by Callender's Cable & Construction Co. Ltd.

Source: H.M.S.O.

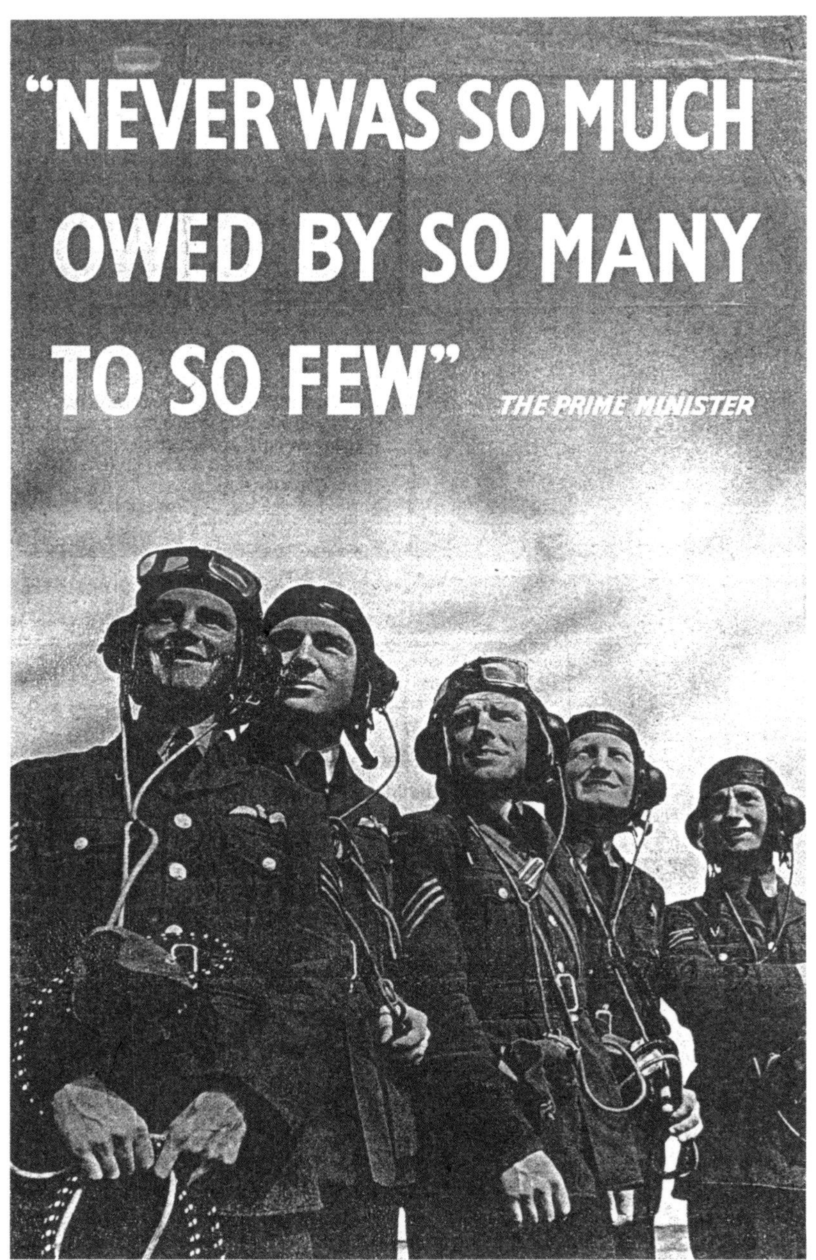

Source: H.M.S.O.

Called to Arms

CHAPTER 3

249 Squadron and the drums of war

With the relentless advance of the German war machine across Europe the fall of France seemed inevitable. Whilst the land-based situation was parlous, in the air it was pitiful. Four Hurricane squadrons of the RAF had been based permanently in France since October 1939, forming a part of the British Expeditionary Force, operating under appalling service conditions, constantly changing airfields —sometimes just landing strips — and short on replacement aircraft and spares. They were fighting a valiant, but increasingly hopeless defensive situation against the tide of numerically superior German forces, their numbers seriously depleted and disarrayed.

Anticipating the inevitable and eventual isolation of Great Britain in the conflict and the expected increased hostility of the seemingly unstoppable Luftwaffe, the Air Ministry decreed an intensive programme in the resurgence of fighter squadrons, for what was seen to be the most critical phase in the country's history. This was to be known as the 'Battle of Britain' — or what the Prime Minister, Winston Churchill was to term 'their finest hour'.

One of the reactivated squadrons selected was No 249, under the command of Squadron Leader John Grandy (later Marshal of the RAF, Sir John Grandy) to be based at Church Fenton. Ideally located some 200 miles north of the Luftwaffe's main offensive targets, it afforded a facility for uninterrupted training — and later —the rehabilitation of decimated fighter squadrons following the debacle in France.

Historically, No 249 was originally formed towards the end of the 'Kaiser's War' deployed mainly in anti-submarine activities off the Scottish coast, operating from a base in Dundee from August 1918 until disbandment in 1919. After fourteen months of existence, the squadron had to wait until the next major crisis in Britain's modern history before the story was continued.

Consequently, in 1940, the unit was to again participate with distinction in the conflict against the might of the German Air Force, quickly earning the reputation as one of the finest fighter squadrons in the RAF. Armed with the magnificent Spitfire, they trained with great enthusiasm and zest, and soon attained a high standard of flying efficiency. However, their enthusiasm was temporarily dashed when their aircraft were taken away for service in the hard pressed south of England. Their malaise, fortunately, was shortlived as brand-new Hurricanes appeared on the scene, fitted with the new Rotol three-bladed variable-pitch airscrews, and a detente between the pilots and these excellent, sturdy aircraft quickly developed. They flew hard, and they flew well in their training programme, ably supported by their two Flight Commanders, Flt. Lts. Kellett and Barton, and a superb ground staff to keep them flying. John Grandy was constantly on the lookout for the best available pilots, with 'guts, flying ability and skill'. Without doubt, Nick could meet the requirement, with good measure, and was transferred from No 72 on 15 May, newly promoted to the rank of Acting Flt. Lt. on 1 June with duties as Flight Commander.

As a young, inexperienced Pilot Officer, Tom 'Ginger' Neil (later Wing Commander) recalls: *'Nick was a tall, rather dishevelled, extroverted young man with dark unruly hair, sometimes resembling a brush. I soon came to know him well — in fact it was difficult not to know him well. A most congenial character in the nicest possible way, he was a self-confessed expert on most things, an amusing talker, mimic, and could be wound up quite easily. Once provided with a drink he could be almost guaranteed to produce good, clean entertainment for hours on end. He instructed me well on the essential disciplines of the Spitfire. Don't, repeat don't, let the engine boil: taxi quickly — but not too quickly!' The Spitfire, as you will have noticed, has small wheels and if too much brake is applied she'll go, and even if she doesn't go over completely the airscrew will probably be damaged and ruin the reduction gear. Don't forget, when taxi-ing, to jink the aeroplane — the view over the Merlin is hopeless so the nose has to be constantly yawed to gain any kind of view. Anyone* not *doing this will be liable for the double chop!*

On take-off, watch for the swing to the left, and never push the nose forward to improve your visibility, otherwise it's a certainty that the airscrew will finish up in the Octopus Den — and replacement. Once in the air you'll find that she flies like a dream, light on the controls and the elevator as sensitive as hell. Oh yes, coming in to land the hood isn't likely to open above 180 — bad design if the truth be known. Always take-off and land with the hood open — always!! Otherwise — no problems. Wheels down below 180 and make a curved approach for best visibility, down flaps at 140 or less. Not above otherwise they won't come out, or possibly damaged. Be careful with the brakes, and don't boil the bloody engine!'

And so he went on — explaining every known hazard in glorious detail. My morale began to take a distinct dip — surely the Spitfire couldn't be all that difficult to fly? Nick was delighted when we were detailed to Acklington for air towing practice against drogue targets. He stressed we should put up a good show for the natives, and spent some time instructing us towards this end. We approached Acklington in a fairly loose formation but tightened up as we swept over the airfield. Following our impressive fly-in we spread out and positioned ourselves to land in a series of three in close formation — a real 249 exhibition. We approached the strip, flying alongside Nick's right side and working very hard to keep formation

—watching his every movement. We cleared the hedge, concentrating hard, and telling myself not to over-shoot my leader, he disappeared from my line of vision as I overtook him. On landing I brought the aircraft to a stop, and turning my head was amazed to see Nick's Spitfire reposing sadly on its belly in the middle of the field. He had been so engrossed instructing us to land that he forgot to lower his own undercarriage. Needless to relate, poor Nick had an embarrassing time in the mess that evening. For two days we fired against the drogue, shooting from all quarters —but I did not hit the target once. On 10 June we returned to Leconfield, to be informed that we were to lose our beloved Spitfires to the depleted squadrons in the south. They were to be replaced by the sturdy Hurricane. With mixed feelings, but in no way depressed, I flew my Spitfire for last time on 1 June. The Hurricanes arrived the day after, and following a short period of familiarisation I quickly developed a rapport for the aeroplane, which, although not as fast as the Spitfire, had many compensatory features which I liked —a very robust gun-platform.

On 9 July we departed for Church Fenton and despite his tendency to authoritarianism on occasion, we became good friends.

We flew together many times, but notwithstanding the fact that he was my senior and section-leader, was not above acting irresponsibly when the mood took him. His wife Muriel lived near the station, and one bright morning we were practising specialised formation flying over their home. I was flying on the inside of a tight formation of three Hurricanes. In a slow climbing turn almost from ground level, he was watching me intently and reduced speed until my aircraft almost fell to stalling speed. I shook my head vigorously at him but he persisted in carrying out the manoeuvre, until my Hurricane fell away at some 800 feet into the first twitch of a spin. I immediately withdrew and flew back to base, infuriated and verbally blasting Nicolson and his peculiar brand of fun ! Back together again at Church Fenton we had a most blazing row, and I lost my temper with him. However, Nick was not one for feuds — which was lucky for me.

The first 'kill' of the squadron occurred on 8 July when a Ju.88 intruder was shot down by 'B' Flight whilst patrolling the North Yorkshire sector. First spotted near the coast as it sought to escape the defences, it finally fell to the guns of 249 (PO Parnall, PO Beazley and Sgt. Main). The pilot of the Ju.88 Oberlt Meier, died at the controls, the other three members of the crew baled out, one of them landing at Aldbrough, near Darlington, close to the farm of Mrs Nora Caldwell. One of the farm workers had seen the German airman land, and hurried to the farmhouse to warn Mrs Caldwell, arriving breathless and agitated, gesticulating wildly with his arms to the sky. She quickly grasped the situation and tried, unsuccessfully, to telephone her husband at the local Home Guard office. She then sent the farm worker to fetch the police, and looking across the field saw the German limping towards the farm, realising that it was too late to fetch one of her husband's shotguns. Without hesitation, but with her heart pounding, she walked to the airman and boldly told him to raise his hands. Not able to understand her demands, he simply stared at her until finally, through gesticulations, raised his hands in surrender. Mrs Caldwell noticed that he wore a hand-gun in a holster around his waist and demanded that he hand it over to her. After what seemed an interminable length of time, he unbuckled the belt and handed it to her.

The German was very young and tall, and seemed to be on the point of collapse after his recent ordeal. The police arrived shortly afterward and took him into custody. Mrs Caldwell was later awarded the OBE for her bravery and initiative.

Earlier in the chapter relating to No 249 Squadron at Church Fenton, Squadron Leader Grandy refers to one of his Flight Commanders, namely Flt. Lt. R G Kellett. Before joining the service he was a stockbroker and known in the squadron circles as 'Boozy' — an affectionate soubriquet, not entirely justified. He owned a vintage Rolls-Royce which was used by all and sundry as a general runaround about the station — the '3-cylinder jallopy'. Kellett later left the squadron to command the newly formed No 303 (Polish) squadron. He recalls a particular incident in the wartime operation of the squadron — in his own inimitable words: *'It was a day in June 1940 and the second-in-command (himself) was in command. The cloud base was a low 200 feet and it was raining hard — a condition unknown in the 'Hitler weather year of 1940'. We assumed no action that morning, but the telephone rang with orders to patrol Hull at 20,000 feet, to which the reply was —don't be silly, no squadron could fly through 20,000 feet of cloud in formation —and where could they land? Answer —nowhere, you have parachutes! Reply — if that is so I volunteer to go with two of the best pilots, but the squadron —no! Fifteen minutes later the telephone rang again, and the NCO says that the AOC accepts your offer —proceed. So Flying Officer Nicolson and Pilot Officer Smithson were detailed to fly with the second in command. They took off and were in cloud almost at once. At 12,000 feet the control warned us of balloons over Hull, obviously they did not know how balloons operated. However, they came out of cloud at 20,000 feet into bright sunshine and a white and level cloud base below. Sure enough, there was the enemy about two miles to the south and we went as fast as possible to attack. The enemy dived into cloud, not to be seen again. The three aircraft returned north over Hull to continue the patrol over cloud — then a thermal tunnel appeared, the sun shone on Flamborough Head — too good to ignore! The aircraft went down the hole and broke up over the sea at about 100 feet, doing about 400 mph. Slowing down a turn to the right with Nicolson in the cloud, and the leader a few feet from the sea. The Flight just managed to cross the cliffs south of Scarborough and land at Catfoss — a closed RAF station. We landed in the quagmire and taxied onto the tarmac. A good breakfast followed, all having had a most exhilarating sortie.'*

249 and the Battle of Britain

On 14 August a signal was received in the early hours instructing the squadron to depart immediately for Boscombe Down to support the hard-pressed fighter squadrons of 10, 11 and 12 Groups in the south. Despite the concentrated efforts by Fighter Command, many Luftwaffe bombers were getting through the defences, causing considerable damage and havoc.

Rumour had it that the move south was to be a short, temporary one of some seven days. Consequently there was feverish activity throughout the squadron, and around noon they were ready to move. Twenty Hurricanes took off —the ground crews and baggage following later by the slow-motion transportation of an ancient Bombay and Imperial Airways Hannibal.

After the well ordered and relatively easy-going atmosphere of Church Fenton and Leconfield, the resonant tension of Boscombe Down was noticeably evident when they arrived around 1.30 pm. They occupied the south eastern area of the airfield, with gaggles of Hurricanes randomly dispersed, and refuelling. There was mountains of baggage and equipment awaiting collection and obsolete old bombers dispersed around the airfield boundary. John Grandy quickly made a call to the Operations Centre at nearby Middle Wallop, returning to report a chaotic scene there; smoking bomb craters, burning hangars and buildings and wrecked aircraft, near desolation caused by marauding Ju.88s. The day closed with a distinct atmosphere of confusion, uncertainty and apprehension. The squadron was now in a state of 'readiness'.

16 August proved to be a hot, sunny day, with a cloudless sky and slight haze, which Luftwaffe pilots favoured. Their targets were shipping, ports and airfields in West Sussex, Kent and Hampshire. On the Isle of Wight, Ventnor radar station was rendered inoperable by Ju.87 Stuka dive bombers. An emergency mobile station proved to be ineffective in operation. the naval station at Lee on Solent was attacked resulting in severe damage to hangars and the destruction of several Fleet Air Arm aircraft, despite the interception of No 213 squadron, who made a desperate dash from their base at Exeter.

A large formation of Ju.88 and Bf. 110 fighter bombers carried out a lightning foray on the naval airfield at Gosport. No 234 Squadron was vectored to intercept the raiders, but failed to make contact. The raid cost the lives of several servicemen and heavy damage. Elsewhere, Tangmere and its satellite airfield of Westhampnett were raided by a force of Ju.88s approaching from the east, destroying hangars, workshops, the officers mess and the sick quarters. Three ground crew were killed when the hangar door fell on them. A surprise attack on Brize Norton, Oxfordshire, a large training station, destroyed hangars full of aircraft. Some 40 aircraft were lost and a number of casualties caused.

That day the Luftwaffe carried out over 1,700 bomber sorties for the loss of 42 aircraft, whilst the RAF suffered 22 fighters shot down with the loss of eight pilots killed.

249 Squadron had been resident at Boscombe Down, Wiltshire, for only two days before they were pitched into the holocaust. At 1.05 pm 'A' Flight comprising three Hurricanes, under the command of Flt. Lt. R A 'Butch' Barton, were detailed to patrol the air space between Ringwood and Poole. Three of the Hurricanes (Red Section) were commanded by Flt. Lt. Nicolson, as Red One, in GN-A (P.3576), whilst PO M. A. King was Red Two, in GN-F (P.3616), an aircraft normally flown by PO Tom Neil, Squadron Leader E. B. 'Whizzy' King completed the trio flying as Red Three in P.3870. 'Whizzy' was a supernumary seconded to the squadron for battle experience prior to taking command of No 151 fighter squadron at Rochester.

'A' Flight's investigation for the reported German raiders soon bore fruit. Nick was the first to spot the formation of three Ju.88 in the direction of Gosport and he reported this to Barton, who immediately detailed him to break away and engage at close quarters. The Ju.88's were flying lower than their patrol height of 18,000 feet and as he drew closer he observed a squadron of Spitfires close in and quickly despatch the offending Hun aircraft. So much for that. Nick again changed course and started to climb to rejoin 'A' Flight. With the sun behind them Red Section were bounced by marauding Hun fighters. They never knew what hit them, and within seconds two of the Hurricanes, Red One and Red Two, were devastated by enemy cannon shells whilst Red Three was badly damaged.

Editor's note. This encounter is recorded in the prologue using Nicks own words which he broadcast on BBC radio on 6 September 1940, so no further comment is necessary on this aspect.

Red Section, and Nick in particular, had been caught in the fatal fighter trap —indoctrinated into fighter pilots since the days of Albert Ball, Mannock and McCudden in World War One:— 'watch out for the Hun in the sun'. Martyn King's Hurricane was critically damaged and he managed to bail out, but suffered cruel luck on his descent. At a height of some 1,500 feet his parachute collapsed plunging this young officer to his death. He fell onto the lawn of 30 Clifton Road, Shirley, Southampton, and died in the arms of a local resident who had seen him descending. He was buried at Fawley cemetery on 21 August, aged just 19 years. The reason for the failure of his parachute will never be known for certain. The Air Ministry stated that the parachute was damaged by enemy action when he was shot down, whilst other versions contend that he was attacked by enemy fighters whilst descending —or was he fired on by our own over-zealous ground forces in a state of nervous hysteria — a not uncommon practice at this critical period.

COMBAT REPORT FROM FLT. LT. NICOLSON TO HIS COMMANDING OFFICER, SQUADRON LEADER JOHN GRANDY, FOLLOWING THE ENGAGEMENT

Received 23.8.40

Royal Air Force, Boscombe Down, Amesbury, Wilts

Dear Squadron Leader,

Thank you very much for your kind letter and meanwhile I feel it would not be remiss to deal in detail with those few hectic moments.

I was proceeding with Red section in the squadron formation, when I noticed three enemy aircraft some distance away to the left. I informed 'Butch', who told me to go and investigate. As however the three unfortunates ran straight into 12 Spitfires long before I got in range, I turned round to rejoin 'Butch', climbing from 15,000 to 17,500 feet so that I could catch him when I saw him. As I approached Southampton I heard Yellow leader shout "Tally-ho, one mile to port," and immediately turned off to join in the scrap, at the same time reaching for my map. As I was opening my map I was struck in the cockpit by four successive cannon shells; the first of which burst on the hood; the second in the reserve petrol tank, which immediately fired; the third on my left foot. Upon hearing the first bang, I had stuffed the nose down and turned hard right, and as the flames came back pulled my feet up on to the seat. I noticed, to my astonishment, during the course of this dive a Me. 110 diving at approximately the same angle and converging with my course — I opened fire at approximately 200 yards and fired until I could bear the heat no more. I am not prepared to swear whether my trigger button was at 'safe' or 'fire' but I do know the sight was switched on. If the guns fired the expenditure of ammunition there would have been approximately 1,000 rounds. Four separate eye-witnesses from the ground however, confirm this as a victory. The '110' zig-zagged as soon as I opened fire, although this may have been due to the rear-gunner sighting me, and shortly afterwards ceased zig-zagging and steepened its angle of dive. I see no reason to believe, however, that it was in any way out of control, and I jumped at this point, striking my head on the roof! I tore the hood open and jumped again only to be brought back by the straps! I pulled the pin and jumped a third time, kicking the 'stick' with my left foot as I did so, leaving the plane like a cork from a champagne bottle. I did not pull the rip-cord for some 5,000 feet, not wishing to be shot, and owing to my excess speed — I left my helmet on. This saved my face. I felt all my limbs on the way down and found there were no bones broken though my thighs, hands, eyes and calves were badly burnt and my left shoe seemed badly shot up. When 50 feet up, just before landing, an enthusiastic individual loosed off both barrels of a 12-bore into my buttocks, this added to my comforts! I am glad to report that I am well on the mend, but it looks as if it's going to take a long time.

All the best to you, sir, and the boys and every success you so richly deserve.

Yours sincerely,

(Sgd) J B Nicolson, Flt. Lt.

Intelligence Report

To: HQFC Intel.

From: 11 Group Intel. Serial No 7805 16.8.40

Intelligence Combat Report

No and type of enemy aircraft: Several Me109s and 110s

Time attack delivered: 1445 hours approximately

Place attack was delivered: near Romsey

Height of enemy: 17,000 feet

GENERAL REPORT: Flight Lieutenant Nicolson (Hurricane 249 Squadron) now in Southampton and South Hants Hospital reports:

I was leading my section in a squadron formation. There were three enemy aircraft some distance to the left. Leader ordered me to investigate but 12 Spitfires engaged the formation before I could get within reach.

I turned to rejoin squadron climbing from 15,000 to 17,500, heard attack signal from leader and was immediately afterwards struck in cockpit by four successive cannon-shells damaging hood, firing reserve petrol tank and damaging my leg and thigh.

I immediately pulled my feet up on to the seat and at the same time I put nose down and dived steeply, turning right four Me.110s diving at same angle and converging. I opened fire at approximately 200 yards and continued firing until I could not bear heat any longer.

I then abandoned aircraft with difficulty and after dropping some 5,000 feet pulled cord — I was shot in buttocks, just before landing. Eye witnesses on ground state that Me.110 zig-zagged and dived steeply after I had opened fire.

This report sent on Flight Lieutenant Nicolson's behalf by Squadron Leader Grandy.

Squadron Leader Whizzy King was indeed fortunate not to have suffered any physical injury during the attack, but his Hurricane was badly damaged. Breaking away from scene of destruction he managed to nurse his stricken aircraft back to base, arriving in a highly agitated state, talking excitedly about the need for an improvement in tactics. On 21 August he was given the command of No 151 Squadron based at Stapleford, and during a combat with Bf.110's near North Weald he had his airscrew shot off but managed to land safely. Whilst on patrol on 30 August, the squadron led by King engaged a force of Hun escort fighters. His Hurricane V. 7369 was shot down and crashed in flames and burned out in Temple Street, Strood. Squadron Leader King was killed, aged 29, and buried in Highgate Cemetery, St. Pancras.

Following the engagement of the 16 August over Southampton, Nick parachuted into a field at Millbrook, a suburb of Southampton. His physical condition was serious, having sustained extensive third-degree burns to his hands and body, wounds from enemy cannon shells and shattered perspex from his cockpit canopy. His tunic was still smouldering, the flames having been extinguished by the wind as he baled out from his blazing Hurricane. As he prepared to touch down, with hardly a breath of air to disturb the parachute canopy, he was subjected to small-arms fire from over-zealous ground forces. Later several pieces of lead shot were removed from his right side and buttock.

The author spent a considerable time investigating, interviewing and corresponding with claimant witnesses to this irresponsible act, which is now established local folklore. A Court of Inquiry was later held 'in camera' to establish the true facts which were never revealed to the public, and all participant witnesses sworn to secrecy. Unofficial findings indicating a summary court-martial were never substantiated.

It is interesting to record that in a report to his Commanding Officer, Nick stated that "when 50 feet up, just before landing, an enthusiastic individual loosed off both barrels of a 12-bore into my buttocks, thus adding to comfort". This he reaffirmed to Muriel and friends later.

Whilst the attack on Red section, and its tragic consequences, was operative, Muriel Nicolson was far away in her home at Kirkby Wharfe, North Yorkshire. Now in a state of advanced pregnancy, she had been taking lunch with her sister when suddenly she had a premonition that all was not well with her husband and contacted the Station Headquarters at Boscombe Down. She was informed that Nick was a casualty, but not the extent of his injuries.

One of the first people on the scene to attend to Nick was a doctor, accompanied by his nurse, Sister Edna Brown. They had been on their round of visiting when they saw Nick descending on his parachute. He was some distance away, but they stopped the car and made their way towards him. Sister Brown describes the incident in a letter to Muriel later. *"He was most anxious about his face, saying that he was never proud of it — but Muriel likes it." I thought it was such a human touch.*

The skin was off his nose but I was able to reassure him that the shape was the same ! His lashes had been singed off and one eye-lid injured which made it uncomfortable, and it was best to keep his eyes closed so he knew me only by voice. The doctor had given him a small dose of morphine to lessen the effect of shock —though not enough to put him right out, of course. Yes, I am afraid that the LDVs made a terrible mistake. They were all young men and anxious to do the right thing. I feel that their minds must have been on the things that happened in Holland when the Nazis landed by parachute, and I am sure it must have upset them terribly when they realised what they had done —a thousand mercies that the harm was not worse. He seemed to be floating down as gently as a piece of thistledown, the parachute opened beautifully and there was not a mark on it. We thought he would be alright and we were bitterly disappointed to find him with burns. We had chased him over fields, through barbed wire and nettles and it was not easy to judge where he would land. His calmness and bravery was simply wonderful, and he seemed to me like the very essence of the RAF — his first thoughts were for his wife and the coming baby — and if his plane had come down clear of houses. These boys of the Air Force are superhuman, crusaders they have been called, and rightly so! He said that he was determined to get back to you.''

In the BBC transcript of the encounter with the 110 he mentions observing a cyclist as he approached the ground. Some quarters state that this was a butcher boy on his delivery round, and when he saw a group of LDV surrounding Nick, laying on the ground with severe burns and wounds, he asked a Sergeant ''did you do this?''. When he replied that he had done so, the boy physically attacked him and a fight ensued, only to be stopped when a policeman arrived on the scene. It was said that an ambulance arriving to take Nick to hospital was used to take the Sergeant away for his own safety. The authenticity of this incident has been investigated —but without any confirmation. It was said by one correspondent who had a relative there at the time, that since meat was on ration at this time no butcher boys were necessary! Perhaps there is some credence to this statement.

The policeman mentioned was PC Eric Coleman (later Superintendent), who was on duty at Shirley police station as an air raid was in progress. He was told that two parachutists were descending and was issued with a Lee Enfield rifle, and proceeded by bicycle to the area. He found that the parachutist had landed in a field at Millbrook and there were a number of people around him. There was no shooting by anyone at this time. Going to the airman, who was obviously English he observed that he was conscious but very badly burned. His first concern was to get him to hospital but he insisted on dictating telegrams to his wife and Squadron Commander. To his wife he said: *''Shot down. Very slightly hurt. Full particulars later. All my love. Nick.''* He was fully aware what was going on and even corrected him for spelling his name wrongly. By this time someone had produced a stretcher and there was a lorry in the field with its driver. He was put on the stretcher and loaded onto the lorry. An ambulance arrived (one of the wartime type) and the person in charge of the ambulance wanted Nicolson moved from the lorry to the ambulance. As the injured man was quite comfortable he would not let him be moved, but told the lorry driver to go straight to hospital, which he did, with the PC riding on the footplate to ensure no hold-ups on the way.

There was no gunplay at any time whilst he was there, insists the Constable, and the only time that he heard mention of a butcher boy was from Mrs Nicolson during a later conversation. As far as he knew, there was no Home Guard taken away in an ambulance.

On arrival at the Royal South Hampshire Hospital, Nicolson's condition was critical and he was given 24 hours to live. Muriel Nicolson confides that he was measured for his coffin. It was sheer will-power and expert medical treatment that pulled Nick from death, and following extensive surgery for burns and wounds he gradually began to recover. At this point the long arm of coincidence played a part in his destiny. A serving nurse at this time Sister Beatrice Jagger, who hailed from the Yorkshire hamlet of Biggin, some three miles from Nick's home, remembered the episode well. *''He was very brave and persevering towards his very serious burns and wounds, but always cheerful and full of youthful antics. When the hospital authorities realised that we both came from the same part of the world, Nick was immediately moved downstairs to my ward to make him feel more at home and aid his recovery. His eyes were bandaged for a fortnight. I remember Mrs Nicolson ringing up from Yorkshire with the news of their newly-born son, James Gavin. The nurses held the instrument whilst he talked.'' Muriel Nicolson says, 'We owe a deep debt of gratitude to the excellent care and skill of the medical staff, especially Sister Jagger —she simply mothered him''.* Sir Harold Gillis, the surgeon-in-charge working in association with Sir Archibald MacIndoe, the prominent plastic surgeon, remarked on Nick's extraordinary recuperative powers as 'nothing short of miraculous!' Whilst the wounds he sustained to feet and legs healed quickly, the severe burns to his hands where most of the flesh had been destroyed, was slow to progress. He was transferred to the Royal Air Force Hospital Halton, near Aylesbury, for specialised treatment.

Nick's former No 72 Squadron Commander, Squadron Leader Ron Lees (later Air Chief Marshal, Sir Ronald Lees) recalls an interlude with him whilst at Halton. *''Nick was just one of the boys — as we all were. He was always mad keen on the Victoria Cross, and knew all the 1914-18 recipients, how they won the decoration, where, when, etc, and the more recent ones granted. When I saw him in Halton, he was recovering from burns and injuries sustained in the battle —and the shots received from an individual's 12-bore shotgun on re-arrival in the UK by parachute. Part of the ward's entertainment was when the nurse picked out shotgun pellets during his dressing. The first time he was allowed out, I accompanied him. We caught a bus to the local town and we had a few beers, and then went to the cinema, followed up with a few more beers at the popular 'local'. I found it extremely difficult and most embarrassing holding a glass so he could drink and putting a sandwich to his mouth. At the end of the evening we made our way back to the hospital, and he wished to urinate. He argued, then pleaded that I remove his lower covering that he might do so. Like all awards of this magnitude, there were inevitably some criticisms from the 'fighter world' that this award was not justified. With his deep love of the Victoria Cross and the scores of people that had won it, these criticisms must have hurt him tremendously. After Halton l did not see him again.''*

What befell the Hurricanes Red 1 and Red 2 when they were abandoned after the debacle over Southampton has been the subject of conjecture for many years. The two aircraft fell within a short distance of each other. One location was in an open field at Lee, near Romsey, between the Salisbury - Southampton railway line and the A.3057 highway. Much valuable work has been undertaken by various aviation archaeologists throughout the country, especially in the southern counties, in the identification of long-buried aircraft. However, in some cases the identification of aircraft depends on small fragments, engine number plates, etc. being handed back from souvenir hunters who witnessed the crash. Recently a Rolls Royce Merlin engine plate was handed in from the crash at Lee which established without doubt the origin of the aircraft, which was P.3576 — Nick's aircraft GN-A. Thus, by elimination, the other aircraft crash at Rounhams, a suburb of Southampton, was identified as the one flown that day by PO Martyn King (P.3616). This aircraft was allocated to PO Tom (Ginger) Neil who was 'off state' ie, not on flying duty roster 'state of readiness'. He resented anyone else using the Hurricane and always inspected the aircraft after this happened. When he heard of the resulting crash from the engagement and the loss of his aeroplane — dear old GN-F — he was sad, but jolly glad not to have been in it!

The fate of the Bf.110 disabled by Nick in the encounter is unconfirmed, after a lapse of 50 years. Nick himself reported the aircraft heading out to sea in its dying moments. The Observer Corps reported sighting an unidentified aircraft crashing into the sea off Calshott about this time, and since there were no land-based enemy aircraft reported crashing in the vicinity that day it would be reasonable to assume that this was the Bf.110 that Nick shot down.

Some historians claim that Red Section was attacked by Messerschmitt Me.109s. This is possible but most unlikely for the following reasons:

(a) Nicolson's Intelligence Combat Report states categorically 'four Me.110s' in close proximity after the attack

(b) Nick again quotes 'chasing the 110' from the transcript of the broadcast that he made on the BBC (see prologue)

(c) In the personal letter to his Commanding Officer, Squadron Leader John Grandy, Nick again refers to 'a 110 converging with my course while diving'

(d) From the operational standpoint, the 109 was a very short range aircraft and rarely seen further west and inland of the Isle of Wight. The 109s of JG53 operating from the Cherbourg peninsula and as far away as Rennes would not have the range to get there, and would be detailed to accompany their bombers — the JU88s and 87 Stukas — at a much reduced speed. Fighter escort duties drawn through a line west of Southampton were carried out by 110s and it is highly unlikely that if there were 110s present on marauding sorties there would not be 109s deployed doing the same job. Moreover, and to give further credence to this argument, three 110s were shot down by 249 Squadron on 15 August — the day previous to the Nicolson incident — in the Romsey area when only a short distance from the position of the Red Section affray. Also, according to reports available later, on 16 August the attack on Gosport (the one that 249's 'A' Flight was about to investigate) was carried out by Ju.88s and 110s. The five Ju.87s which attacked Ventnor in the Isle of Wight about the same time were almost certainly escorted by 109's of JG53, three of which were shot down over, or near the Isle of Wight around that time. There were no reports of any other German fighters infiltrating inland, and Ventnor, situated on the southern tip of the island, is some 25 miles south of where Nick and his section were attacked.

Nick always referred to a '110 being in front of him' and this was confirmed by witnesses at the time. Squadron Leader Whizzy King, who was the only member of Red Section to survive the attack and return to base, never referred to 109s in his report, and in conversation, of the event. Certainly no one within the squadron at the time was ever aware that 109s were involved. Operating from Boscombe Down, they never encountered them further west than the Tangmere area.

On 1 September, 249 moved to North Weald where the severely battered 56 Squadron was relieved for a period of rest and refurbishment. 249 arrived with about 18 Hurricanes, all with code letters GN, whereas 56 Squadron had less than a dozen — some of them severely shot up — all with the code letters US, and all equipped with VHF radio. Because 249 had only the less efficient HF radio it was considered expedient to exchange aircraft rather than spend several precious days changing the radios. Consequently, 249 flew the serviceable aircraft of 56 Squadron for a period of about three weeks, but since a number of these were subsequently lost in combat and replacement aircraft were flown in, they returned gradually to a full complement of their own letters — GN. It is not surprising, therefore, that there are photographs of the period which show Hurricanes operating from North Weald with designation US which were, in fact, on the strength of 249 Squadron. Some incidents arose, eg, when Sgt Pilot Palliser ran out of fuel whilst flying a US-coded Hurricane and force landed in a field near Brentwood, sometimes to the confusion and embarrassment of the less well-informed latter-day historians.

It had been some time before the true facts of Nick's engagement with the Bf. 110 had become known to his colleagues at Boscombe Down, first reports being that he had been shot down and received a volley of buckshot in the buttocks on the way down by parachute. After all his good advice to others, he had fallen victim to the renowned 'fighter trap' — first time out! Knowing Nick's ability to tell a good story, they awaited his version with some amusement.

Later, when all the facts of the battle came to light when told by Squadron Leader John Grandy, who had taken down Nick's combat report in hospital, there was genuine sympathy for the tremendous ordeal and injuries that he had sustained and they were impressed by his bravery. Muriel, his wife, was unable to visit him in hospital because of her physical condition and imminent confinement.

On 17 August the squadron was visited by Group Captain HRH the Duke of Kent, accompanied by Group Captain, later Air Marshal, Sir Ralph Sorley. Perhaps it was sheer coincidence that the visit was timed only one day after Nick's engagement with the Bf.110?

At the Halton hospital it was certainly coincidence that Nick's friend Hiram Smith was also there, and among other things, they compared notes on the wager that they had regarding the first Hun to be shot down whilst serving with No. 72

Squadron. Nick conceded that he had lost the bet and duly paid up, handing over a cheque for £1.00 which he had crossed 'War Account'.

The treatment for burns at this time was the liberal coatings of gentian violet, of a bright purple colour, with no resultant improvement to the patient's appearance. They were allowed a good deal of mobility, and one lunch time they went out to the local pub. On their return, they went to their respective wards and subsequently Nick said that he met several distinguished looking civilian gentlemen coming down the stairs as he went up. No doubt they were affected by his appearance and enquired what had happened to him. In his usual uninhibited manner he gave them a graphic account of his encounter with the Bf 110, his blazing Hurricane, his delayed bale out and the destruction of the Hun aircraft. What Nick didn't know until some time later was that the leader of the civilian group was the Secretary of State for Air, Sir Archibald Sinclair. Nick said that the members of the party seemed very interested and concerned on hearing his account.

By October 1940, it was apparent that a momentous air battle had taken place over the skies of southern England, with many acts of supreme courage and self-sacrifice by the pilots of Fighter Command, to be known in perpetuity as the Battle of Britain. For three months the might of the Luftwaffe had given 100% commitment to the destruction of the Royal Air Force and its airfields, and the ports and shipping of the English Channel. London — and its valiant civilian population had refused to submit to the holocaust created by raids — and so the 'Battle' petered out with the advent of winter. The losses of both men and aircraft had been heavy on both sides, and now the Luftwaffe was to change its tactics and attack by night.

Reichsmarshal Goring's decision to discontinue the air bombing of Fighter Command stations in the south was perhaps the biggest single strategic error of the war, giving the Royal Air Force much needed breathing space to build up again its severely depleted service, to fight again in the critical days ahead.

249 Squadron in action

No 249 Squadron at North Weald - 1940

Source: Tom Neil

From left to right: Pilot Officer Burton —killed on 27 September when he courageously sacrificed his life in combat when he rammed a German bomber; Flight Lieutenant 'Butch' Barton — a Canadian; Pilot Officer Lewis —South African; Pilot Officer Crossey —South African, died; Pilot Officer Tom 'Ginger' Neil; Pilot Officer Beazley; Squadron Leader John Grandy (later Marshal of the RAF); Pilot Officer Barclay —killed in North Africa, 1942; Pilot Officer Lofts.

Source: Andrew Saunders

Squadron Leader John Grandy with Nick and Adjutant Lohmeyer at Church Fenton, No. 249 Squadron

Source: Tony Vasco

Me. 110 fighter-bomber

Nick at R.A.F. Hospital the Palace Hotel, Torquay, just before the award of the Victoria Cross.

No. 249 Squadron re-union, 1990 Standing, left to right. Cyril Hampshire, Peter Rowell, Charles Palliser, Tommy Thompson, George Stroud, Ronald Symth and Tom Neil. Sitting L/R. 'Mac' McConnell, Wally Evans, MRAF Sir John Grandy, and Jerzy Solak (Polish). The Squadron bar is little changed since those epic days of 1940.

No. 249 Squadron (plus 50 years). This re-union was devised and organised by Mr. Trevor Williams (historian extraordinaire). Left to right: John Bentley-Beard, Cyril Hampshire, Peter Rowell, Tommy Thompson, George Stroud, Tom 'Ginger' Neil, MRAF Sir John Grandy, Charles 'Tich' Palliser, Jerzy Solak (Polish), Wally Evans, Ronald Smyth, and 'Mac' McConnell. Anthony Hutton's beautifully restored Harvard trainer in background standing in for 249 Hurricane.

CHAPTER 4

The 'unearned' Victoria Cross

At this point in the war there had been no recipient of the Victoria Cross within Fighter Command, although 12 had been awarded to the other Services —four to Bomber Command, five to the Army, and three to the Navy. Hiram Smith speculates on this point by saying, "*I assume that the Air Ministry had been on WW1 criteria whereby a score of 45 enemy aircraft destroyed brought the award of the Victoria Cross. But in 1940 no-one had achieved such a score so what should be done about it? How could they decide on new criteria and, if so, how many VC's should be awarded — and to whom ? Obviously a very different problem but the solution could be to find an outstanding individual example, and they found him on the stairs at Halton Hospital ! Some weeks later we met again at the Palace Hotel Torquay, which had been appropriated as a RAF hospital. Once again we had been to town at lunch time with several friends and upon returning to the Palace Hotel and entering the front door Nick was called over to the desk in the hall. I sat down on a settee at the opposite end of the room, and a few moments later a completely shattered Nicolson collapsed beside me and thrust a piece of paper into my hand. It was a telegram and the message started off: 'His Majesty King George VI etc.' and I thought it must be a joke. Reading on, it promulgated 'the award of the Victoria Cross to Flight Lieutenant J B Nicolson'. As I finished reading the message Nick turned to me and said 'Now I have to go and earn it'.*

When he had sufficiently recovered his composure Nick sent a telegram to his wife, Muriel at her home in Yorkshire, it read: *'Darling. Just got VC. Don't know why. Letter follows. All my love. Nick.'* On receiving the news she immediately rang and congratulated him on the tremendous award. (She later confided that when Nick was about to open the telegram he thought that he was to be court martialled!) The news of the award quickly circulated around the hospital and the place was alive with good cheer.

The origin of the award came from Wing Commander Victor Beamish, Station Commander at North Weald, No 249 Squadron's new base from 1 September. It was for a Distinguished Flying Cross.

He was not, however, aware that the Commanders-in-Chief of the three home operational Commands — Portal, Dowding and Bowhill — had received a letter from the Air Member — Personnel dated 29 August expressed in the following terms:

The Secretary of State told me in a recent conversation with him, that the King expressed surprise that the recent exploits of the Royal Air Force had not produced more recommendations for awards of the Victoria Cross.

Whilst it is appreciated that you will naturally submit recommendations for any acts of gallantry performed in your Command which merit this prized decoration, both the Secretary of State and I, as Chairman of the RAF Awards Committee, know that you will not submit any which tend to lower the very high standard of bravery which is rightly required. This is apparent from the description of the deeds which have earned the three awards which have so far been made to the Royal Air Force during the course of the war.

It is, however, at the request of the Secretary of State that I write to inform you of the interest which His Majesty is taking in this matter.

(Signed) E L Gossage

Dowding had passed this intelligence on to his Group Commanders, and two days after the submission by Beamish, on 28 October, Air Vice-Marshal Keith Park, AOC No 11 Group, added this note to the Beamish citation under 'Remarks of Air Officer Commanding':

Flight Lieutenant Nicholson showed exceptional courage and disregard for the safety of his own life by continuing to engage the enemy after he had been wounded and his aircraft was burning.

For this outstanding act of gallantry and magnificent display of fighting spirit, I recommend this officer for the immediate award of the Victoria Cross.

Dowding concurred, and on 3 November, under Remarks of Air Officer Commanding-in-Chief, he added in a handwritten note:

I consider this to be an outstanding case of gallantry and endorse the Recommendation for the award of the Victoria Cross.

In passing the recommendation to the Permanent Under-Secretary, The Chief of the Air Staff, and the Secretary of State, Air Commodore R D Oxland, the Director of Personnel Services, explained how the original recommendation for the DFC had been upgraded by Dowding and Park. He also explained another singular circumstance — the usual review by the RAF Awards Committee had not taken place due to the indisposition of the Chairman, the Air Member for Personnel: 'I have given the recommendation careful consideration and it appears to me to be less strong than those which earned the VC for FO Garland and Sgt. Gray, Flt. Lt. Learoyd and Sgt. Hannah. The following factors, however, need to be taken into account . . .' (he then gave the references of the previous letters to Air Member Personnel (Air Marshal Gossage) . . . 'in the circumstances an award to Flight Lieutenant Nicolson might, perhaps, be approved.'

RECOMMENDATIONS FOR HONOURS AND AWARDS

Christian Names: James Brindley Surname: NICHOLSON 28A

Rank: Flight Lieutenant Number: 39329

Nationality: British.

Command or Group: Fighter Command Unit: 249 Squadron

Particulars of the meritorious service for which recommendation is made, including date and place.

During an engagement with the enemy on 16th August, 1940, in the neighbourhood of Southampton, Flight Lieutenant Nicholson's aircraft was hit in the cockpit by four cannon shells; he was wounded by two of the shells, whilst another set fire to his gravity tank. Just as he was going to bale out he sighted another enemy aircraft, a M.E.110, which he attacked and shot down into the sea. As a result of staying in his burning aircraft Flight Lieutenant Nicholson sustained serious burns to his hands, face, neck, and legs. Flight Lieutenant Nicholson has always shown great enthusiasm for air fighting, and this incident shows that he also possesses courage and determination of high order.

ME 109 according [illegible]

State what recognition is recommended. **D.F.C.**

State appointment held or how employed. Flight Commander, 249 Sqn:

Signature of Commanding Officer,

F. V. Beamish .... Wing Commander

Date:- 26th October, 1940. Unit: R.A.F. Station, NORTH WEALD

REMARKS OF AIR OFFICER COMMANDING:

Flight Lieutenant Nicholson showed exceptional courage and disregard for the safety of his own life by continuing to engage the enemy after he had been wounded and his aircraft was burning.

For this outstanding act of gallantry and magnificent display of fighting spirit, I recommend this Officer for the immediate award of the VICTORIA CROSS.

K R Park

Air Vice-Marshal, Commanding,
No.11 Group, Royal Air Force.

28th October, 1940

REMARKS OF AIR OFFICER COMMANDING-in-CHIEF:

I consider this to be an outstanding case of gallantry and endorse the Recommendation for the award of the Victoria Cross. H.C.T. Dowding A.C.M.
3rd November 1940.

Source: Public Records Office, Kew

Both the Permanent Under Secretary and the Chief of the Air Staff concurred the Oxland Minute. The next day, 7 November, the Secretary of State was *'glad to submit this decoration'.*

Life in the Palace Hotel convalescent home was brightened by the formation of an improvised orchestra and concert party, known as the 'Swanee Whistle'. With his outgoing, gregarious personality and musical inclination, Nick was a great support to the concert party which was assembled by RAF officers in the hospital for their own entertainment, and for the amusement of the more badly wounded. Nick soon proved his prowess on the Jews harp and the tin whistle, and contributed his musical talent by crooning as part of the 'harmony boys' group. Meanwhile, his physical condition continued to improve and he was able to play squash and one-handed golf.

16 November was a proud day for the Nicolson clan, marked by the birth of their long-awaited first born child, a son, to be named James Gavin. Muriel matched her husband's earlier news by sending a telegram from the nursing home which read *'Nicolson Junior baled out safely at 9.15 this morning'.*

Nick was naturally overjoyed by the momentous news and his new role of father and his one thought was to join them at home in Kirkby Wharfe. This was not to be for some weeks yet, as prescribed by the hospital authority.

The Mayor of Torquay, Councillor C G Price, invited Nick to the platform of the Pavilion to be introduced to the townspeople of the town, but he was so completely overawed by the sense of occasion that when it came to addressing them he was completely tongue-tied — a rare moment for the normally loquacious Nicolson. However, the enthusiastic crowd cheered themselves hoarse. *'I have never met such a modest man in the whole of my long public career'* said the Mayor later.

Journalist Charles Graves remarked, *'It isn't easy to ask VC's how they earned their decoration, but I am sure that Flight Lieutenant Nicolson hadn't the slightest idea that anything was coming his way. His exploit had happened on 16 August and he had forgotten all about it, hence his shock at receiving the telegram. I was telling him that he would have to expect to make a number of speeches when he returns from convalescent leave. He replied that he had no intention of making any speeches whatever. He went on to say that there was some ridiculous story around to the effect that his nickname was 'the Professor'. 'For the record, I have always been known as 'Nick' — and have never been known as anything else! ' Recanting of his excellent care whilst in hospital in Southampton, one night, during the period when his eyes were bandaged, he asked the Sister what she looked like. She replied that her hair was mousy, her figure was tubby, that her nose had got bent whilst playing lacrosse, she wore horn-rimmed spectacles, and had a mouthful of teeth! Nick said that he had only one memory of her — that she had a hand like a block of ice, which was very desirable in his position when his shot of morphia only lasted 50 minutes.*

We later went to London shopping and we called at my tailors ostensibly for a VC ribbon. He said that there was no room under his wings so they had to be raised whilst the ribbon was being selected for size etc. The ribbon in those days cost 6d

(2½ new pence) and the miniature cross of the VC cost ls 6d (7½ new pence). On the way by train to London I asked him where he proposed to purchase his VC ribbon. Somewhat embarrassed, he said he didn't know, but I put his mind at ease when I suggested he leave it to me as I knew London pretty well. After all, it is a nice point how to phrase the question to a strange shop assistant, or even a tailor, 'have you by any chance got a piece of VC ribbon', or 'I would like a bit of VC ribbon, please'. If you are the actual recipient of the decoration you are bound to be a little self-conscious, embarrassed or nervous.

On Nick's first leave from hospital it was the intention to make his way to York station, and beyond, as unobtrusively as possible. Having been granted a few days 'compassionate leave' shortly after the birth of James Gavin, this had only served to strengthen his resolve for a speedy and permanent hospital discharge. He was met in York by Muriel and a few intimate RAF friends and they proceeded to Kirkby Wharfe, where they had a family reunion and celebration party. Nick's desire to have a quiet and restful leave was not to be. Outside there gathered a barrage of pressmen and photographers, which he was very reluctant to meet, but with 'gentle persuasion' from Muriel and two friends to 'go and get it over', he proceeded to face the cameras and answer numerous questions. Success breeds success it is said, and Nick was no stranger to this axiom, for the population of Kirkby Wharfe was now awaiting his pleasure to congratulate him. Also, the children of the local school at Ulleskelf were arranging a special party in his honour. Mr Archie Holmes, host of the local Ulleskelf Arms, Nick's friend, had arranged a darts match, supported by two ribbon-bedecked bottles of champagne and local brewed Yorkshire 'bitter'.

The Tadcaster Rural District Council had been busy arranging a Celebration Ball at the Riley-Smith Hall to be followed by a presentation of a specially sponsored portrait. No peace for Nick in the foreseeable future!

Congratulatory telegrams arrived by the score from friends and associates in the RAF, delivered by 70-year-old pensioner Harry Harlow, who later said that he regarded the extra work as an honour.

The Archbishop of York (Dr Temple, later Archbishop of Canterbury) in a handwritten letter said, *'Congratulations and best wishes — all Yorkshire is very proud of its connection with you'*. The Headmaster of his old school at Tonbridge wired, *'School flag flying in your honour today. Come and see us as soon as you can'*. Mr and Mrs William Riley-Smith (owners of the well known Tadcaster brewery) was one of the first telegrams to be received, saying, *'Congratulations on valiant effort'*. One message which Muriel received was from Nick's great-aunt, Mrs Bladsworth, aged 80, who had loaned her bridal veil for Muriel's wedding. Nick's former Squadron Commander, Squadron Leader John Grandy, wired the message, *'Atta boy, Nick. Congratulations on magnificent news'*.

To add to the homecoming celebrations in the hamlet of Kirkby Whare, the christening of nine-week old James Gavin Kendall had been arranged at St. John's the charming old country church for the following Sunday. The Reverend R C Capel Cure (Vicar of Ledsham) who took part in the wedding service as a friend of Nick, conducted the ceremony. He had been an observer in the Royal Flying Corps during the Kaiser's War. The congregation included many personal friends and relations of the parents, among whom were Mrs Dorothea Nicolson, Nick's mother; his two sisters Lesley (one of the godmothers, who was wearing the uniform of the Women's Auxiliary Air Force) and Jeannie, wearing ATS uniform; and a younger brother Charles Gavin Nicolson, who was shortly to join the RAF. Also present was Mr Arthur Kendall, Muriel's father. Nick's father, Leslie Nicolson was unable to attend due to indifferent health, as was Muriel's sister.

The godfathers were Service friends of Nick, Flt Lt Hiram Smith, and Squadron Leader Morris, who was unable to attend due to illness, his proxy was Squadron Leader Millson. The second godmother was Mrs Watson Hall, of Scorborough Hall, Beverley.

Whilst on leave from the RAF hospital in Torquay, Nick attended a succession of parties, fetes and gatherings given in his honour. One very busy evening began with an informal tea-party at the Mansion House, York, accompanied by Muriel. They left the party to call in at their home to see baby James in Kirkby Wharfe, who was in the care of a nurse. Having decided that all was well with Nicolson Junior they called in at the Poppleton Sugar Factory Sports Club, just in time to see the presentation of a hand-embroidered tablecloth to the Lord Mayor (Alderman W Horsman) by Miss M Kitchen, aged 18. She had been working until a late hour for several days in order to have the tablecloth completed for the occasion, which was special in that it had the signature of four members of the British Cabinet on it, one in each corner and Nick's in the centre. The four Ministers were Winston Churchill, Sir Archibald Sinclair, Secretary of State for Air, Major C R Attlee, Deputy Leader of the House of Commons (later Prime Minister) and Mr George Hicks, Minister of Works. The tablecloth was to be later handed over for a special auction to raise money for the Red Cross.

In a later speech, the Deputy Lord Mayor, Alderman Dobbie, praised Flt Lt Nicolson saying *'that if it was not for courageous young men like him on land, sea and in the air we would have been brought to a position like France and made a vassal state of Germany'.*

The congratulations and accolades continued until it was time once again to return to hospital in Torquay.

It was on a sick leave shortly afterward that Muriel and Nick were meeting friends in the Station Hotel, York, that they received a telegram summoning them to be present at Buckingham Palace for the Investiture of the Victoria Cross by His Majesty, King George VI on 25 November, a matter of only a few days away.

Nick's family were quickly informed of the arrangement, not knowing whether he would be able to take his wife and mother with him. Still hoping, but not knowing, he arrived in London and took them with him to the Palace. Included in the family circle were his sisters Lesley and Jeannie, both in uniform of the WAAF and ATS respectively, who had special leave for the occasion. He nervously asked if the family could wait inside. The palace official said that he would ask the King if he would like to meet the family, and returned shortly to say that the King would like to do so. They were ushered into a private sitting room amid many corridors where the King waited, wearing naval uniform.

As soon as Nick had been presented to him, the King walked over to the rest of the family and shook hands. He smiled and said 'You're in the Services too' when he observed Nick's uniformed sisters. He looked at Nick's hands, still dark-skinned and not yet normal from the severe burns sustained earlier, and asked if they were getting better.

The King did not ask if he wanted to fly again, but doubtless the answer would have been an emphatic 'yes'. Little did he know at this moment how decisive an influence the King had had in the promulgation of the award. Although extremely proud to be so honoured he had the increasing conviction that somewhere within the Air Ministry hierarchy he had somehow been 'selected' for the award. He always maintained that, in his opinion, he had not earned the distinction and that there were others who deserved it more.

The King stayed chatting for a long time after he had handed over the Victoria Cross in its leather case. There was no formal pinning on.

There was evidence of broken windows in the quadrangle and the filled-in bomb crater. Muriel remembers — *'The King told us where the bombs had fallen and joked over the broken windows, saying that they were more of a liability than an asset when bombs were being dropped. He was a charming man, and one had to meet him to realise what a strong personality he really had. He made us feel almost at home in that grand tapestry-hung room.' When the interview was over, and the party was being escorted back along the corridors, one of the Palace aides came hurriedly to Nick and stopped them and said, 'The King would like you to have this!'* It was a small cardboard box for the medal case, which had been forgotten in the excitement. The five Nicolsons left the Palace for a celebratory meal at the Grosvenor Hotel.

Reunion at Royal South Hants Hospital (Sister Jagger, seated, second from right)

Nick recuperating from burns

Source: Imperial War Museum

'The Swanee whistle'

Source: Imperial War Museum

Nick with jews harp at Palace Hotel Hospital

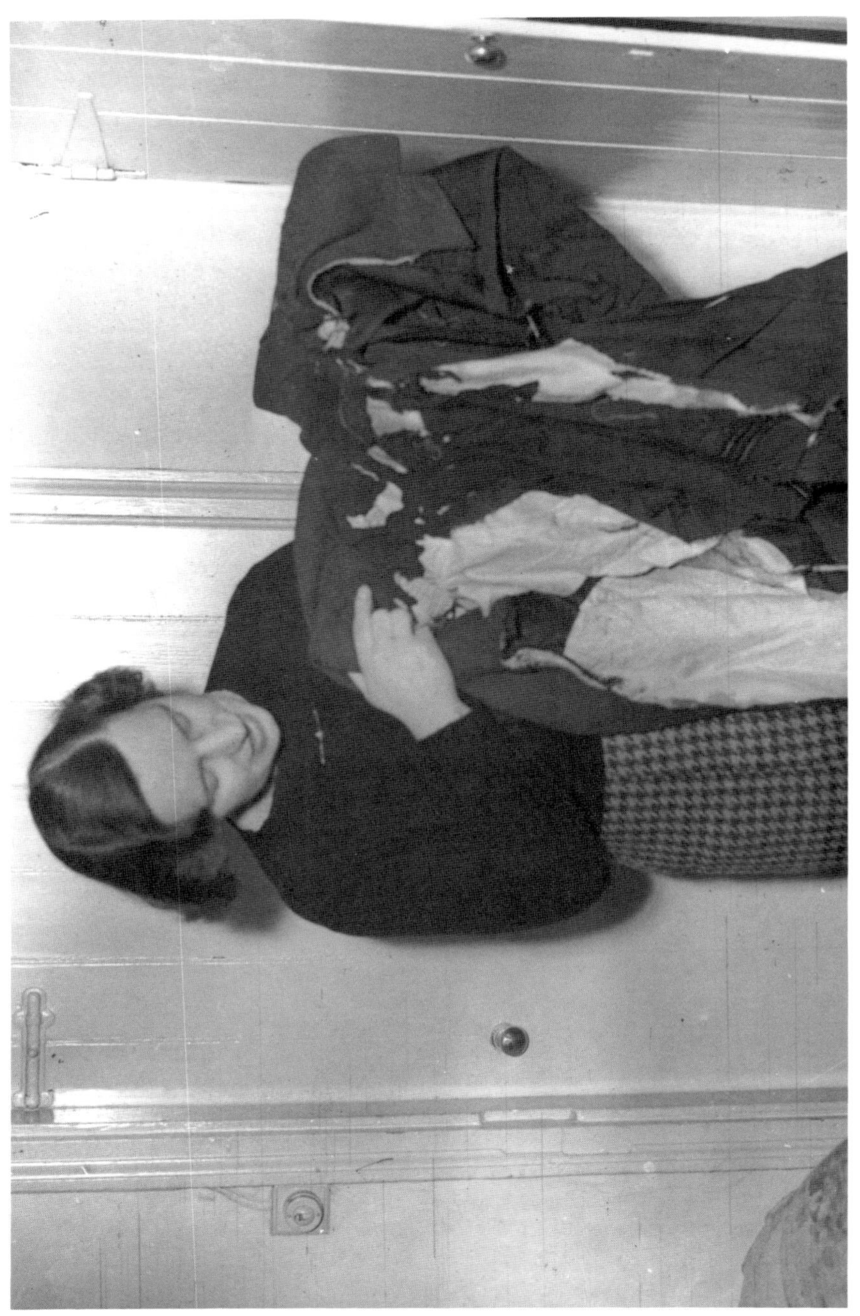

Muriel Nicolson showing Nick's burned uniform

Recuperation at the Palace Hotel, Torquay

Congratulations at Palace Hospital, Torquay

Source: Chaz Bowyer

The new fighter VC with his hallowed award.

Mrs Muriel Nicolson reading the congratulatory telegram of the Victoria Cross, November 1940

Muriel with congratulatory VC telegrams

The Nicolsons with baby James Gavin

Bathtime for James.

Proud parents relaxing in Kirby Wharfe

The Christening

Reception at York with the Archbishop of York

Nicolson at his 'local', the Ulleskelf Arms

Source: Daily Express

Nick talking to Belgian refugee Leon Fievez, from Mons, whilst on sick leave at Kirkby Wharfe.

Source: Andrew Saunders

Flight of Hurricanes on patrol

CHAPTER 5

No 54 Operational Training Unit and the Turbinlite Flights

In February 1941, Nick reported for what he hoped would be his final physical check by the medical board. He was declared fit, with the exception that his left hand had not reached the accepted degree of mobility required for operational flying, but graded suitable for administrative duties. He was discharged and posted to RAF Church Fenton as Chief Ground Instructor with the newly formed No 54 Operational Training Unit (see 'Fighting' Church Fenton).

At this juncture in his young life there was a mental impasse. He had, by a combination of sheer will-power, the finest of medical skills, and perhaps most importantly, the Grace of God, survived the most devastating of personal experiences and physical tribulations. Despite his phenomenal good fortune it seemed that he was not destined to follow his great love —operational flying. The award of the Victoria Cross hung over him like some veritable Sword of Damocles. He repeatedly asked himself if he was worthy of the great honour that had been bestowed on him, which since its inception in 1856, had been granted only to the select few. Were there not others more worthy than he to receive this distinction

Muriel confirmed on more than one occasion, to the author, the great turmoil created by the award — *'it was like a two-edged sword that both filled him with pride and troubled him to a point of obsessiveness'*. She later asked Lord Dowding why there had been granted only one Victoria Cross to Fighter Command during the war, to which he replied, *'The action must be seen and witnessed by others, in particular by a member, or members, of the unit. In the case of a multi-crew aircraft it was comparatively easy to qualify this condition, but with a single-seater fighter aircraft of independent capability this presented a different set of circumstances.'* (This is not a verbatim statement but accurate in context when a time span of some 50 years is taken into account —Author.)

He was desperate to return to flying and had the aptitude for the fighter role. In the final analysis he had to face the reality that the left hand was to be permanently immobile, clawlike and never likely to unclench, but, as he told Muriel on several occasions, *'it's not pretty but it can still handle a throttle. After all, Douglas Bader flew with tin legs!'* There was only one solution to the dilemma and that was to fly operationally again — and prove his worth. Four years training should justify more than one Hun shot down!

No 54 OTU was commanded by Wing Commander R L C (Batchy) Atcherley DFC, who, in company with his twin brother David, were both distinguished officers and both to later attain Air Rank status. Their family home was at Fulford, York, and they were good friends of the Nicolsons. Batchy had approached Nick before he was medically discharged to help him build up the Unit, which was situated conveniently near to his home at Kirkby Wharfe, and although it was not a flying job he was pleased to accept the posting — if only on a temporary basis.

No 54 OTU was a completely new concept whose primary function was to train pilots and radio operators in conjunction with the AI (aircraft interception) radar system, to meet the night operations of the Luftwaffe bombers and intruders, who were wreaking havoc with night operations of the Operational Training Units throughout the country. The main aircraft on charge were operational-rejected Blenheims Mk IV, Oxfords, Defiants and the station Magister; later Beaufighters Mk I for advanced training. On 10 August 1940 it was decreed that the sector station of Church Fenton be transferred from the operational control of No 13 Group to No 12 Group, the Air Officer Commanding being Air Vice-Marshal R E Saul MC DFC.

The Unit suffered heavy casualties in trainee crews and aircraft due to inexperience of the pilots, the shortfall of standard of the aircraft —and German night intruders.

Apart from the occasional flip in the station 'Maggie', Nick's duties were strictly routine which became more irksome as time progressed. He repeatedly lobbied his superiors for an operational flying posting. His persistence eventually paid off when he was transferred to Hibaldstowe — a satellite station of Kirton Lindsey, where the new Turbinlite system was being developed to combat the devastating night attacks by the Luftwaffe bombers. The motley counter-measures provided by stop-gap nightfighters had proved ineffective, notwithstanding the use of Airborne Interception (AI) equipment, which was still in the early stages of development. Alternative methods of locating and destroying the enemy raiders were now urgently needed.

A practical suggestion was propounded by Wing Commander W Helmore, who was then attached to the Ministry of Aircraft Production, which was simple in conception — effectively a flying searchlight which would enable the raiders to be seen by our defences on the dark winter nights, which would take over from AI at the crucial moment of interception. The 'flying searchlight' would be carried by an aircraft of sufficient dimensions to accommodate the necessarily large light, and of comparable performance to the attendant night fighter. The technicalities of producing and housing such a light were enormous. The General Electric Company's research laboratories at Wembley finally produced the light to Air Ministry specification rated at 150 kilowatts, having a 90cm para-elliptic glass mirror powered by batteries. The unit was finally ready to install in an aircraft, the Douglas DB-7 Havoc II at this time being taken on for service with the RAF seemed to be the ideal aircraft for the duty — although a single Mosquito was adapted for experimental trials. The accompanying night fighters were usually Beaufighters, and to a lesser extent, the Hurricane.

On the night of 28-29 March, Bomber Command sent a force of aircraft to bomb the historic town of Lubeck, leaving the Baltic town devastated by fire. The enraged Hitler retaliated by ordering the bombing of similar British towns which were to be known as the infamous Baedeker Raids, named after the pre-war tourist guides from which the targets had been selected. The Turbinlite Flights, numbering ten units in all and ranging from as far afield as Acklington, Northumberland, to West Malling, Kent, were granted operational status on 28 February, 1942. The Baedeker Raids, directed at Exeter, Norwich, York and other cities, should have presented an ideal opportunity to the Turbinlite Flights to prove themselves operationally, but in the event they turned out to be ineffective for a variety of reasons — despite the tremendous efforts of the crews for unity. Nick's tour of duty with the Turbinlite Flights included time with No 7 BAT Flight at Finningley, 1451 Flight at Hunsdon and 1459 Flight as Commanding Officer at Hibaldstowe. He was still confined to administration duties, and on one occasion had to report the lack of security measures at Hibaldstowe — which did not enhance his popularity with his seniors.

By September the days of the Turbinlite Flights were numbered. Statistics for the six months April to September showed the following results.

BEAUFIGHTERS VERSUS TURBINLITES

	Detections	*Visuals*	*Combats*	*Destroyed*	*Probables*	*Damaged*
Beaufighter (with AI Mk 7)	215	95	59	28	11	14
Turbinlite Havoc	38	11	5	1	1	2

As early as June, the Commander in Chief, Fighter Command, Sir Sholto Douglas, had written a memo doubting the efficiency of the concept when compared with the success of conventional night fighting techniques. Despite the possibility of an improved Turbinlite Mosquito armed with its own 20mm cannon the idea of illuminating enemy aircraft to counter night raids was finally abandoned in favour of the eminently more successful AI radar systems being developed. The Turbinlite Flights were disbanded in January 1943.

During his time with the Turbinlite Flight, Nick was asked to participate in the Leeds Warship Week, the object being to raise £5,250,000 for a replacement for the aircraft carrier Ark Royal. He made a rousing inaugural speech on the Wednesday of the week, which was Royal Air Force Day. He congratulated the citizens for the previous total of £3,345,000 and emphasised the great need for the target to be reached, saying, *'if you have tried your best —then try harder. We cannot go up into the sky and shoot down the enemy with Tiger Moths, nor can we fight against the Panzer divisions with a pop-gun. See that you provide not only a big Ark Royal but a little one as well.'* He then set the target indicator and later took the salute when the RAF parade marched past. A magnificent effort in fund-raising was made by Leeds businessmen and ordinary citizens — including school children.

Bristol Blenheim Mk IV

Source: Air Research Publications

Havoc aircraft with Turbinlite in nose

Douglas Havoc with nose Turbinlite

Source: Air Research Publications

Royal Air Force Day Tuesday, 3 February 1942. Squadron Leader James Nicolson taking the salute at march past of Airmen

CHAPTER 6

The Burma Campaign

As a consequence of the infamous attack by Japanese naval aircraft on the American base of Pearl Harbour in December 1941, the two countries were at a state of war. This attack was the culmination of years of planning by the Japanese Imperial Staff for the conquest of the Far East, which comprised China (her old enemy), Siam (now Thailand), Malaya, and the sub-continent of Burma and India. The British and American authorities had for some time suspected this ambitious intention but had given the possibility a low priority rating. By contrast, the Japanese had placed great store on the occupation of Burma as a gateway to the rich spoils of India, notwithstanding the considerable natural resources of Burma — oil and rice.

The British authorities set up a plan — codename Matador — as a counter to any potential invasion of Malaya and its resources of rubber latex, but it proved to be unsuccessful in operation due to the serious shortcomings in the standard of defence since most of the aircraft on charge were approaching obsolescence.

On 23 December 1941 the invasion of Burma by the Japanese commenced. Sixteen bombers with a fighter escort attacked the port of Rangoon, and according to official records, were engaged by 16 Brewster Buffalo and 14 Curtis Tomahawk fighters, the encounter resulting in the loss of nine enemy bombers and one fighter against the loss of two Tomahawks in the air and the destruction of nine allied fighters on the ground. A second raid shortly afterward produced a similar proportion of losses — approximately four to one. There were heavy civilian casualties due to insufficient air raid precautions.

The summer rains of 1942 came and went, and the autumn passed with its attendant steamy heat. In Calcutta, the RAF fighter pilots with their Hurricanes waited 'at readiness' for the predicted Japanese bombing raids, using the city's impressive Red Road as a landing strip. The Japanese were some time before they carried out their assault on the teeming capital of Bengal, by which time all but four of the Hurricane squadrons had been withdrawn to support the limited offensive against the Japanese-held island of Akyab, off the Arakan coast, chosen by Field

Marshal the Viscount Wavell as the only move, at this stage, that he could make towards the future reconquest of Burma.

On a moonlit December night the Japanese bombed Calcutta causing slight damage to an oil plant at Budge-Budge. The effect on the civilian population was disastrous, causing a mass evacuation by dawn. In all, 25 raids were carried out by the enemy at night, causing plague and disease fomented by the heaps of rubbish left rotting by the civilians. The Air Officer Commanding in Chief, Air Chief Marshal Sir Richard Pierse, immediately called for night fighters with AI gear to relieve the situation. Flight Sergeant Pring, flying a Beaufighter of Allied Command, intercepted the bombers, shooting three of them down. Four nights later on 15-16 January, FO Crombie destroyed a further two more night raiders, with the effect that the raids ceased from then on.

Singapore fell to the Japanese, resulting in the decimation of British resistance in Burma, and with the capture of Lashio, the Burma Road was ineffective and supplies to China seriously threatened.

An alternative route had to be found quickly. The problem was alleviated by the creation of an aerial highway by the American Air Force, to be known as 'the hump', by which means thousands of tons of essential supplies were transported to Chungking. The flights were dangerous over the little known Patkai mountains where cumulo-nimbus formed in great profusion, the bulbous great masses, if entered, would most certainly shake the wings off a Dakota aircraft with their vertical currents approaching 150 mph, of unimaginable ferocity and force within their gloomy depths. Despite these hazards the 'hump route' was used successfully throughout the war to almost 'bus-service' proportions of one aircraft every ten minutes. 'Calcutta to Chungking non-stop.'

In the space of three months the Japanese forces had negated American power and captured British and American key bases in the south-west Pacific theatre, forcing the depleted and exhausted remnants to retreat into Burma and India. However, there was worse to come. Within a week of Pearl Harbour, the Imperial forces of Japan invaded Burma, a country of mountain ranges running north to south, split by deep valleys and three main rivers — the Chindwin, Irrawaddy and the Salween. To the south, Burma created a barrier between Malaya and India, whilst to the north the majestic, massive, natural barrier created by the Himalaya range — the 'roof of the world' — effectively blocked any easy access to China or India. The climate varies from cyclonic monsoon rains to drought conditions. In the monsoon season it is possible to simulate domestic shower conditions with a bar of soap!

The climatic conditions under which the Allies — and the Japanese — had to operate are worthy of brief study. Rice was not the only prize since Burma was part of Japan's 'greatest land grab in history'. The Burma Road, China's last land link with the Western Allies, was severed and a wedge of mountain and malarial jungle was driven between them. The valley and delta of the Irrawaddy are a paddy-field from which seven million tons of rice can normally be harvested, which ideally suited the rice-eating Japanese garrison. The Allies, who ate a variety of food had to be supplied from faraway India, which meant that the war of supply in Burma was between the parachute and the paddy-field. On the banks of the Lower Irrawaddy were located the oilfields of Yenangyaung, which pre-war had produced annually some 250 million gallons of crude oil. Although the Allies had blasted the installation as they retreated in order to deny the petroleum to the Japanese, it was sorely needed for our own mobility. By occupying the inner basin of Burma, the enemy had the advantage of holding the area least affected by either monsoon or malaria —major afflictions to troops serving in them. The Japanese commanded a far better system of land communication than the Allies at this time. The monsoon is born in the Bay of Bengal in May, creating a wet zone in the north of Burma, and another in the south, whilst the dry zone is in the central part of the valley of the Lower Irrawaddy, which was the main base of Japanese power. Variations of the intensity of the monsoon are governed by the angle at which the cloud strikes the mountains. On the windward slopes generate most of the rain — 500 inches annually at Charapunge, in Assam, making it the wettest place on earth. Whilst at Shillong, a few miles distant but on the opposite side of the range, the rainfall is only 60 inches. When Burma was lost to the Allies, the greater part of their operational activities were conducted either in the hills or on the windward side of them — a definite disadvantage. The monsoon finishes in October, and from then on is dry, and even cold until the hot pre-monsoon season commences from March to May. The Lower Irrawaddy is healthy, the north of Burma is pestilent, and some parts are so malarial that both armies avoided fighting in them. It was the power of the mosquito, and not the enemy that was the deciding factor in operational planning. As the Supreme Allied Commander Lord Louis Mountbatten, later said, 'Malaria has conquered empires and can cripple armies'. It was recorded that 250,000 British casualties were laid low suffering from the effects of malaria and dysentery

The land is mainly thick, lush matted jungle and undergrowth of mammoth proportions, described by many who were serving there as 'the worst country in the world'. Logistically, Burma represents nature at its most belligerent to any army traversing its rugged terrain, complete with all manner of pestilence and hazards awaiting the unsuspecting within the steaming greenery of the jungle. A summation of the conditions encountered would include extreme humidity, prickly heat (which seemed to affect the younger men worse, and even the monsoon downpour seemed to offer no relief), hookworm (in the foot), the 'dhobi-itch' (intense soreness in the crutch), scorpions, and the 'Bombay Canary' (large flies as big as cockroaches which seemed to have a fatal attraction for the overhead cooling fans resulting in splatter over a wide area).

Retreat of the Allied forces in Burma was hard fought, pursued by the relentless and fanatically triumphant Japanese, as happened in Malaya. The advance of the enemy was effectively halted on the Indian border by the monsoon after the last remnants of the British and Indian armies crossed the Chindwin River to take refuge. They immediately reformed and gathered strength for the inevitable reconquest of Burma. The RAF was almost completely devoid of operational airfields, except in India. Under appalling monsoon conditions, the Army sappers built airstrips along the developing Arakan coastal road, and in December, 1942,

No. 224 Group Air Command moved from Calcutta to Chittagong with the remaining Hurricanes and Blenheims. The task of the Combined Air Services was to continue the strategic air offensive and destroy the Japanese Air Forces and all that that implied. Consequently top priority was given to build up the wide diversity of squadrons numerically and with the most up-to-date and efficient aircraft, aircrew and ground staff.

The background of No 27 Squadron was one of mixed fortune. Formed at Hounslow Heath in November 1915, they were bereft of their own aircraft for several weeks, and with a growing complement of pilots had to practise flying in borrowed machines as the opportunity presented itself. By the beginning of February the equipment began to arrive.

These aircraft were the Martynside G100 Scouts, dubbed the 'Elephant' by the manufacturer's design staff because of the nose shape. Henceforth the squadron was to be known as the 'Flying Elephants', the squadron emblem inscribed with the motto 'Quam Celerrime ad Astra' (With all speed to the stars) — and a centrally placed Elephant in relief. The squadron was disbanded in January 1920, but was shortly afterward reinstated as a unit by replacing the squadron No 99 with their own. They flew the sturdy DH9A on 'peacekeeping' patrols against the turbulent mountain tribesmen over India's North West Frontier, until 1930, when the DH9A was replaced by the Westland Wapiti which remained on charge until the outbreak of hostilities in 1939. The equipment was again changed to the Tiger Moth and Hawker Hart, when in October 1939 the squadron was raised to operational status flying Bristol Blenheim Mk I(F) fighters. Whilst serving in Malaya most of their aircraft were destroyed on the ground by the Japanese in a wave of bombing raids. They were detached to Sumatra but were nullified as a fighting unit when the Japanese overran the country (see squadron history at rear of book).

On 19 September 1942 they were again reformed at Amarda Road airfield in the state of Orissa, some 130 miles south-west of Calcutta, and were to be the first of three Beaufighter squadrons which would form a Wing to operate over Burma. The squadron records state:

September 1942. No 27 Squadron formed. Authority formation Order No 287 issued by Air Headquarters, India, dated 3 December 1942, reference 3116/311/Org. The squadron's establishment will be India/703 when the Government of India's sanction has been obtained. The squadron will be under the direct control of No 224 Group.

The pilots and ground crew gradually arrived from the various other theatres of war. Due to Administration error the Squadron Commander, Wing Commander H C Daish did not report until 3 December, having mistakenly been posted to the Middle East to command No 454 Squadron, an Australian light bomber unit. The first two aircraft arrived on 18 November — Beaufighters Mk VI(F) and TF-X, for training and conversion. By 21 December there were 13 Beaufighters on charge to the unit.

The Beaufighter was the successor to the earlier Blenheim and Beaufort marques and was a formidable instrument of war. With its twin Hercules engines developing 1670 horsepower (ideal) it was sometimes described as 'two large engines followed by an aeroplane'. The quiet operation of these efficient sleeve-valve engines soon earned the aircraft the reputation of 'the whispering death' with the enemy. The Beaufighter was no match for the Japanese Zero fighters in aerial combat, but could show them a clean pair of heels when operating at ground level —a feature that the crews of No 27 Squadron greatly appreciated. Normal cruising speed was 170-175 knots at 1800 rpm and -2 pounds boost, but by increasing the revs and boost to 2600 and + 6, a speed of 280 knots in straight and level flight could be attained. It also had a very useful range of 1600 miles. Being of robust construction it could take extensive punishment and had devastating fire-power when armed with 4 x 20mm cannon in the fuselage and 6 x .303 machine guns in the wings. Later marques were fitted with 8 x 3in rocket projectiles under the wings — a veritable flying arsenal ! There is no doubt — as confirmed by several former pilots of No 27 Squadron —that crews who flew Beaufighters on operations found them to be magnificent aircraft, giving them tremendous confidence and sense of pride in the knowledge that they could inflict great damage to the enemy, whether the target be low level attack against Japanese communications, railways, roads, river transport, aerodromes or troop concentrations, as far as 500 miles from base. There was provision for a rear-firing machine-gun in the navigator's position but it was not a success in Burma since it occupied too much of the navigator's space, and allowed excessive cold air to enter the aircraft through the slot in the canopy.

The new Commanding Officer, Wing Commander Harry Daish, did much sterling work to assemble and train the air crews to peak efficiency, and he personally led the squadron's first sortie on 24 December 1942 on a low-level strafing raid against Japanese-occupied Toungoo aerodrome. The same day proved lucky for the crew of Beaufighter EL276, when it crashed at Dum-Dum airfield Calcutta, with no casualties.

On 8 January 1943 the squadron was detailed to move to Kanchrapara, an RAF Maintenance Unit situated 30 miles north of Calcutta. This move was brought about for two reasons: (a) the ground crews were not fully familiar with the Beaufighter due to the rapidity of the squadron formation and operational programme, which resulted in functional problems; (b) serious problems due to malfunction of the 20mm Hispano cannon on operations, when frequent stoppages were experienced. A speedy solution was necessary if the operational status and the standard of morale of the squadron — which up to this point had been high — were not to be affected. Frequent technical discussion with high-ranking officers of No 221 Group were arranged, resulting in visits by Wing Commander Buchanan, Senior Armament Officer, AHQ Delhi, and Flt. Lt. Bourne, AHQ Bengal Engineering. By the end of January 1943 only six Beaufighters were considered of operational standard.

The problem with the gun stoppages was soon diagnosed after exhaustive tests by the technicians — and frustrated aircrew. It was proved conclusively that the trouble was due to 'excess tension on the cannon links caused by slightly oversize cannon shells which had the effect of preventing the cannon shell from releasing from its link when it reached the breach'. All the suspect shells were withdrawn, rebelted and air tested at the Hoglabada air-firing range, in the delta area of the Ganges. Although the cannon stoppage problem had been successfully surmounted, each aircraft had to be calibrated and harmonised, involving the manpower of the whole squadron. There was also problems with the spark plugs, which had to be completely changed, using another type. In order to assuage the morale situation, a 48-hour leave system was instigated, followed by more frequent half-day breaks.

In February 1943, the squadron was detached to Agartala, East Bengal, which was to be their operational station for the next twelve months. The move was carried out in sections by air, road and rail. Agartala was a busy station which came under the tutelage of No 224 Group and No 169 Wing — first under the command of Wing Commander Elsdon DFC (a former member of No. 72(F) Squadron at Church Fenton — see tributes at rear of book), followed by Group Captain Champion de Crespigny.

After only two days at Agartala, 27 Squadron was once again operational, on a ground strafe sortie on the Irrawaddy River. The runway was a single concrete track a mile long which had a pronounced dip of some 15 feet in the middle, which led to occasional accidents to the uninitiated, since any misjudgment by the pilot on landing induced the tendency to become airborne again, despite braking action of the wheels.

Three squadrons were resident there: No 5 Squadron with Mohawk single engined fighters; No 31 Squadron with Douglas Dakotas; and No 27 Squadron, the total number of aircraft being some 50 operational types. The base was protected against Japanese air attack by the Army, and the RAF Regiment had several hundred soldiers for security. The several thousand air force, army and unskilled Indian labourers who made up Agartala were billeted within their own units, dispersed around the airfield. No 27's living and mess quarters were about three miles distant, known as No 1 Camp. Squadron accommodation was divided into three groups —officers, NCO's and airmen, all the buildings were made from local materials —bamboo for the walls and rush-type grass for the roof, and hand-made bricks for the floor.

The sanitary facilities were effective, if austere, and took the form of a hole in the ground some 15in in diameter and 15ft deep. They were ingeniously constructed by the Indian labourers using two bamboo poles, one with a sharpened end to loosen the soil. The other, slightly larger, had a splayed end, which when thrust down the hole collected the soil. By this method the complete hole was fashioned.

Air conditioning —or basically movement of warm air — was provided by the 'punka-wallah', the punka being a woven grass blanket fitted in the ceiling, and given an oscillating motion by means of a rope. Often the punka-wallah was affected by the movement of the punka, inducing a soporific effect on the operator, much to the annoyance of the airman.

Boredom —when not actually flying — was a problem tolerated by all ranks. The Commanding Officer, Wing Commander Harry Daish, recognised this and devised counter-measures, sport playing a big part in the proceedings. The squadron soccer team was formed and played in inter-squadron and inter-Group competitions, but because of the heat, the playing time was reduced to 20 minutes each half. Notwithstanding, at the close of the match both sides were perspiring profusely. The

Daish Cup was introduced by the CO for all inter-squadron matches, and from two competitions played by the aircrew team and the Headquarter team, each won equal laurels. Badminton and archery proved popular — and later pigeon shooting. Swimming was a popular request, but no facilities were available.

There was a well patronised open-air cinema on base which invariably showed films of the 30's. Squadron concerts were organised and on occasion ENSA (Entertainments National Service Association) arrived from the United Kingdom. These were tremendously popular, especially when Vera Lynn, the 'Forces sweetheart' was present — a rare sight to see a white woman, which generated long queues of autograph hunters, and the chance of a word from the Home Front.

Squadron personnel were called upon to give lectures on their specialised subject, whether it be navigation, maths, morse code, etc, relevant subjects for airmen intending a transfer to flying duties. Tuition in the French language and local Burmese dialects did not, for some reason, prove to be very popular.

In the evening, squadron personnel indulged in their own particular interests —reading, playing darts, or simply engaged in conversation over a drink. Flt. Lt. Swift could be relied on to permeate the quarters with the mellifluous strains of 'Dearly Beloved' on his gramophone.

Liar dice was an addictive pastime in both messes, which meant several hours of play — with the unfortunate loser paying for the drinks. Dedicated bridge players could play for days on the same game, before there was a settlement.

Animal pets became part of squadron life, providing entertainment and interest to the squadron at large. Dogs and monkeys were the popular choice —but two Himalayan bear cubs were acquired by PO John Townsend —but he forgot that tiny cubs grow up to be big bears, four feet tall to be precise. They were named Elsie and Rupert and were a great attraction. As a pair they did not present any problems, except when the mating season arrived, and Rupert became difficult to control and restrain on his leash. There was concern that they could attack personnel and inflict severe injury, consequently the hard decision was made to shoot Elsie — a sad day for the squadron.

Flt. Lt. David Innes took possession of a rhesus monkey which he named 'Modu'. Although affectionate towards her master she did not get on with David's bearer, a pleasant, quiet young Indian called Ali, and sometimes sank her teeth into him when the two of them were left alone. Modu — meaning honey — was kept on a long lead which gave her freedom to roam outside the basha hut. One day she slipped her lead and managed to undo the cap of a bottle of aspirins. In the safety of the hut ceiling, she quickly swallowed the contents of the bottle — and passed out. It was several days before she was back to normal!

For any extended leave many airmen made for Darjeeling, 'the Queen of the hill stations', which was at the foot of the Himalayas and some 400 miles to the north of Calcutta, at an altitude of over 6500 feet. The temperature range there was 35-65°F, a very pleasant relief after the steamy atmosphere of Agartala. It was reached by overnight train from Calcutta to Siliguri, at the foot of the Himalayas, the journey being completed by taxi, or narrow gauge, British-built railway. The views from

Darjeeling were magnificent, taking in Mount Kanchenjunga (28,140 feet). On a clear day, 130 miles to the west, the magnificent Mount Everest (29,028 feet) could be seen. It was a popular holiday centre for both servicemen and civilians, with its first-rate hotels, sporting facilities and horse-racing at the Lebong track. Other recreational trips were made to Kashmir, and its capital city of Srinagar, in north-west India.

No 27 Squadron continued its operations, flying low-level sorties against Japanese military targets. Under Group HQ instructions, formations of Beaufighters, in flights of six aircraft were used for the sweeps. This did not suit the tactics or the characteristics of the Beaufighter, and was changed to flights of two Beaufighters, one as leader and the other following behind and 100 yards to port. This tactic soon proved its worth in practice by the element of surprise and made them less vulnerable to detection by the roaming Japanese Zero fighters.

There were frequent losses to the enemy and involuntary crashes for various reasons — damage sustained in action and wounded aircrew. The following log is indicative of the losses suffered from the period February to July 1943.

17 February, 1943 — FO J Townsend and PO Wandless. Raid on Heho airfield, failed to return. Beaufighter C.

21 February, 1943 — Sqn Ldr Illingworth DFC and Sgt Osguthorpe. Low level attack on Frome town, crashed, presumed victims of anti-aircraft fire.

7 March 1943 — Flt Lt McMichael and Sgt Dodd. Failed to return but they survived in prisoner of war camp. Later repatriated.

26 March 1943 — Sqn Ldr Statham AFC, and PO Briffett. Shot down by Zero fighter.

4 April 1943 — Sgts Ensor and Clough (Beaufighter 'V'). Lost, out of control returning from coastal patrol.

26 April 1943 — seventeen aircrews detached to newly formed 177 Squadron at Pharpamau.

17 May 1943 — FO Sturrock and Sgt Heywood (Beaufighter 'O'). Failed to return from train strafing operation. Believed hit by AA fire.

29 June 1943 — Sgts Petch and Thomas (Beaufighter 'A'). Failed to return, no known reason.

7 July 1943 — WO Thorogood and FO Welch. Crashed at base when brakes failed. No injuries.

4 July 1943 — Sgt Johnson and Flt Lt Dinwoodie attacked and destroyed a million-gallon Japanese oil storage tank near the Irrawaddy. Both were subsequently decorated.

In July, Wing Commander Daish was posted to HQ Bengal, Barrackpore, as Wing Commander, Organisation. All the squadron was sorry to see him go.

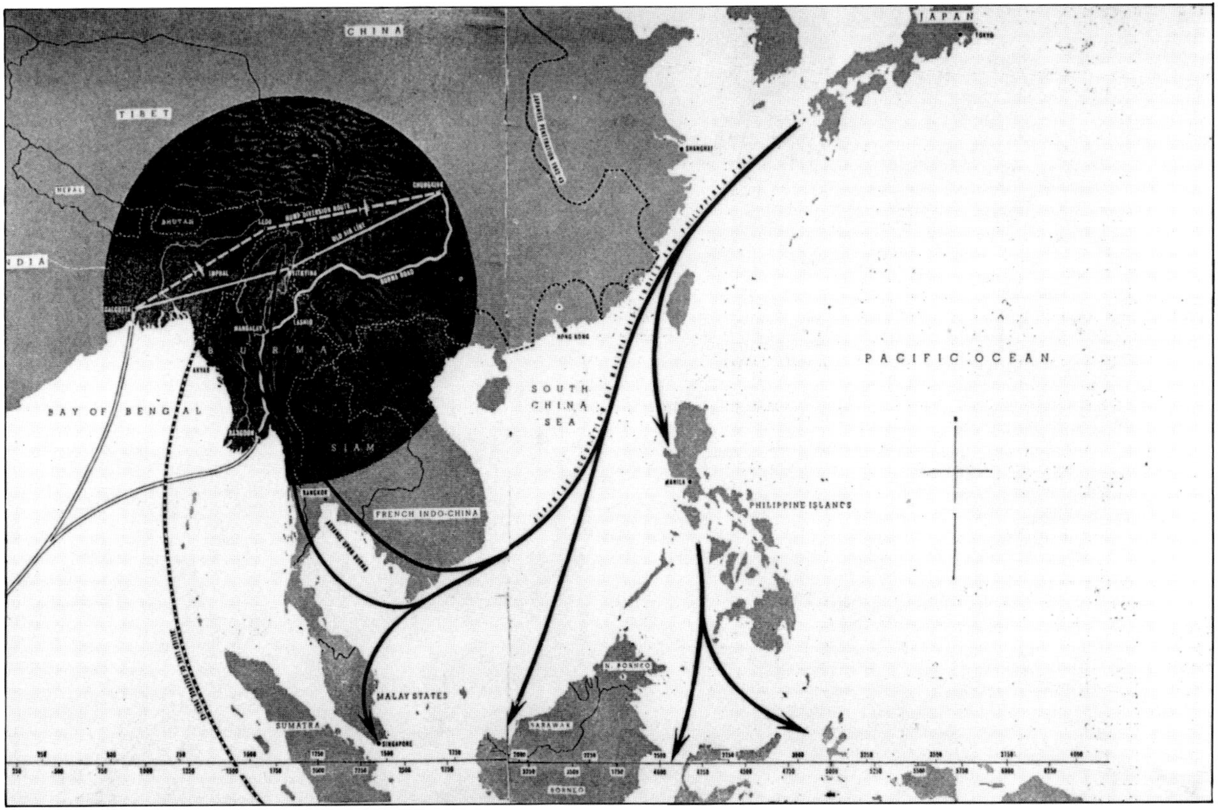

Operational map of South-East Asia

Beaus in Burma

HERE's a piece which we think is of considerable value to Beaufighter pilots flying, or about to fly, in Burma. It deals particularly with flying in monsoon weather and the gen it contains is hot from the griddle—in other words, it's from a recently returned pilot. He has had experience of three monsoons and reckons that his advice is probably the most suitable for Beau X's, which have a comparatively low ceiling and no oxygen.

Flying conditions in Burma are as a whole excellent between October and February. About the only snag is low-lying mist in the early morning. From March to May, however, conditions deteriorate. Heat, bumpiness low down, very bad haze and occasional vicious storms, all seem to gang up on the pilot of a low-flying aircraft and make his life more than somewhat unpleasant.

From June to September comes the south-west monsoon, bringing rain. And when we say rain, we mean rain in a big way, far heavier than anything you've met in England. Moreover, it has great penetrating power, which makes it very difficult to keep your wireless equipment at a high standard of serviceability.

But even heavy rain — most frightening in large quantities — need not worry you. The first thing to remember is to keep your gills closed; there's no need to use hot air. Should the air become too viciously bumpy and so make instrument flying very difficult, go back on a reciprocal. Fierce electrical storms should be avoided; there's no future in flying over Burma with your compass u/s.

The rain doesn't worry Prune.

When over the sea, keep as low as possible, *i.e.,* 300-400 feet, and get under the storm rather than over it. Before going on to instruments, try to fly at 50 feet up and get the altimeter at o feet. This will give you a little to play with and allow for the drop in barometric pressure due to the storm.

Monsoon flying over hilly country is a little more tricky. Anywhere south of Imphal, *i.e.,* over the large majority of Burma, the highest mountain is 10,000 feet. If the weather is sufficiently bad to cause trouble, it will be definitely impossible in a Beau X to climb over it. So try going through at 12,000, giving a 2,000 feet clearance of the highest mountain. At this height, oxygen will not be necessary, and the engines will still give — 2 lbs. at 2,000 r.p.m. In addition, you will be flying well below freezing level, which is about 15,000 feet.

Source: H.M.S.O.

The rain doesn't worry Prune

CHAPTER 7

No 27 Squadron the 'Flying Elephants'

Following the disbandment of the unsuccessful Turbinlite Flights. Nick went home on embarkation leave to Kirkby Wharfe. He later sailed from Liverpool by troopship en route for Bombay, India, and arrived at Headquarters 293 Wing, Alipore, on 15 May as Administrative Officer — a desk job. The yearning to be on operational flying was as irrepressible as ever, and following a series of administrative postings he arrived at Agartala, East Bengal, on 4 August 1943, to command No 27 Beaufighter Squadron. Somewhere down the line he had acquired a border collie. Muriel said that he was a great dog lover, particularly Retrievers.

He lost no time in acquainting himself with the Beaufighter and made his first flight in the afternoon, which was duly celebrated in the mess that evening.

After a short period of acclimatisation and 'getting to know you' period he set out his programme of administrative changes. A new look was given to the squadron with no disturbance to the general activities. The post of Intelligence Officer, Engineering Officer and Signals Officer underwent change, including one or two Flight Commanders.

With the improvement of the weather in August and September the scale of operational sorties against land and river targets was increased considerably — the highest yet. The number of aborted flights was reduced to only seven, and no losses in aircraft or aircrew. The Japanese also took advantage of the improved weather to increase activity in their supply lines, by road, river and rail, with consequent increase in military targets for the Beaufighters.

According to records available, for the period January to the end of September 1943, the summation of Japanese military objectives destroyed, or seriously damaged was:

Locomotives	66
Steamers, motor launches, sampans and other river craft	1495
Road transport, lorries, etc	95
Rolling stock	415

This inventory of destruction did not include attacks on oil tanks and installations, so vital in the maintenance of mobility of any fighting force.

On one occasion at least, the quiet approach of the 'whispering death' paid off, when a Beaufighter completely surprised the proceedings of a Japanese ceremonial parade — possibly Emperor Hirohito's birthday — at Myitkyina, a large Japanese airbase in northern Burma. The parade was devastated by the Beaufighter's cannon fire, leaving a bloody trail of destruction, including a decapitated central flagpole with its shredded 'rising sun'.

Nick's predecessor, Wing Commander Daish, had previous experience in aerial photography before joining No 27 Squadron, and pioneered the use of various experimental cameras for the important role of photographic and visual reconnaissance. The first camera had a 5in f.24 lens which fitted nicely into the nose cowling, and was wired for operation by the pilot. A similar, but larger lensed camera, was fitted within the flare chute for taking rearward facing shots, but this was plagued by condensation problems brought about by traversing routes of differing atmospheric conditions —i.e. mountain coldness into steamy jungle terrain in quick succession. The problem was eliminated by the removal of the glass register plate. The cameras were synchronised to operate in unison with the firing of the cannons, and produced good results.

In September, the newly formed Beaufighter unit, No 177 Squadron, became operational, thus taking some glory from No 27 Squadron as the only Beaufighter squadron operating within No 224 Group. They were based at Fenny aerodrome and the two units co-operated and liaised well together.

On 11 September the very successful team of WO Ron Thorogood and Flt Lt Edgar Welch had a 'highly destructive' sortie when they destroyed the squadron's 100th Japanese locomotive. This sortie was given much local radio publicity —which eventually filtered through to the media of Britain and Australia, and much of the (then) free world. A transcript of the broadcast given on 30 September by All-India Radio, Calcutta, gives a brilliantly graphic description of conditions at this time.

Censored script of broadcast 30.10.43 at All India Radio, Calcutta by FO Welch and FS Thorogood

UN-'TRAIN' THE JAPS

Voice 1: Reading your newspapers during the last few weeks you must have noticed the frequency of the raids by RAF Beaufighter aircraft on Japanese locomotives, trains, railway stations — and in fact all kinds of communications in Burma. This may not seem very important to the casual reader, but it is in fact one of the most vital of our preparations for any assault on enemy-occupied territory. There are very few good railways in Burma, and those that there are are now of very much less use to the Japanese than they were when the enemy had plenty of locomotives to haul his trains. That was before the squadron which has become famous as the 'Trainbusting Squadron' got busy. Only a few days ago this squadron destroyed its hundredth railway engine in Burma, and the score is now well past that mark. Here in the studio are the pilot and the navigator of the aircraft which brought the squadron's score up to the century mark, and they're going to give you their own impressions of the 'busting' of the hundredth railway engine. The pilot who is a flight sergeant, is, by the way, a Yorkshireman whose home is in York, and who used to be employed in a glassworks there before he joined up. He's married and has a six month old son whom he has never seen because the baby was born after the pilot sailed from England last autumn. Flying with him as navigator is a flying officer who was born in Sunderland, but whose home is now in London, where his wife is living. I might add that this pilot and navigator first met at an Operational Training Unit in the United Kingdom. They came out here together and have flown together ever since.

Now here they are to tell you the story in their own words. First of all the navigator will explain how they located the hundredth engine.

FO Welch: Well, before I do any explaining let me say that it was only good luck on our part that we happened to be flying the aircraft which destroyed the hundredth loco. The whole squadron was very keen on getting the 'century' engine and we just happened to be the ones who found it.

To give you a rough idea of the size of our hunting ground I ought to say that our squadron has ranged over a stretch of territory from the coast of Burma to well beyond the Irrawaddy and northwards. I should estimate that we've covered some 200,000 square miles of Burma in our search for locomotives, railway targets and river craft. On this particular trip my pilot and I accounted for eight railway engines. But the one you want to hear about we spotted on a single line track hauling a train of goods wagons and carriages. There were two engines actually, and we 'sailed in' and let them have it with our cannon and machine guns. One of the engines — the squadron's hundredth — belched steam and smoke, and we circled round for the second attack. This time we wrecked the other engine. I think there was no doubt about that, Flt Sgt?

Flt. Sgt. Thorogood: There certainly was not! Both engines definitely had it. The train didn't look too good, either, when we'd finished with it. I'll bet the Japs were surprised when they saw us coming along the railway line scarcely higher than the carriage roofs.

FO Welsh: Yes, I'll bet they were too, and sorry that they couldn't take evasive action!

Flt. Sgt. Thorogood: The Japs are getting very chary about exposing their railway engines nowadays. They do their very best not to be caught napping — but it isn't a very good best. Just after we'd accounted for these two engines we found another one a little further on, and we plastered that one till it belched smoke and flame. Along the 60 mile length of track we covered we found several other engines, too, and let fly at them.

Voice: Did you manage to get away without any damage to yourselves?

Flt. Sgt. Thorogood: *Well no, not exactly. The railway line was like many similar stretches in Burma. It twisted and turned as it wound along a valley into the hills towards Lashio and the line was often hidden by tall trees hanging over it.*

Just after the first attack we ran into heavy anti-aircraft fire at a viaduct, and when we got back I found that shrapnel had struck the plane, but luckily neither of us was hit. The starboard wing was the only place that caught it. The damage wasn't very serious but it meant a bit of repair work for the ground crews.

Voice: It must be difficult to follow a line which is continually twisting and turning?

Flt. Sgt. Thorogood: *Yes, when you're sweeping along at very high speeds it is easy to overshoot a twist in the line — especially if you're keeping your eyes open for hills to avoid. It's important to miss the hills when you're flying very low!*

Voice: I should say so!

Flt. Sgt. Thorogood: *But the navigator helps there of course. He's always tremendously helpful. On this particular occasion there were two aircraft taking part in the attack. Ours was one and in the other the squadron's CO was flying as pilot with a Flt Lt as navigator. Both aircraft flew over the hills from Bengal to Burma. We had to fly through pretty thick cloud for nearly half an hour before breaking into open weather. We crossed the Irrawaddy, and by locating a converging river turned towards the target. We were following the CO's plane just north-east of Mandalay when we spotted the engines I've told you about. The CO saw our attack on the engines and confirmed that both were well and truly hit.*

Voice: Good show! FO you said a moment ago that your hunting ground was pretty extensive; it must be tricky sorting out a target like that in such a large area ?

FO Welch: *Well, it's not always easy. You see, navigation over Burma is a matter of getting hundreds of miles across very rough country to a specific pinpoint and then steering a course to reach the target undetected. You have to catch potential enemy defences by surprise. It's easy to get off the right course when you are flying at very high speed, unless a careful watch is kept. As you can well understand it's essential that the planes should be 100 per cent efficient for these strenuous conditions, and 'I'd like to say a word or two at this point about the men who look after them on the ground. Both the pilot here and myself have a great regard for the ground crew, who work under 'George' — a sergeant who solves any problems which face him when we land. Those problems are sometimes pretty difficult if the aircraft has been hit. He may have to decide whether a damaged component can be repaired or whether it must be written off — and he must make his mind up pretty quickly. He must have some nasty headaches at times. During the monsoon these fitters, mechanics, armourers and so on worked tirelessly, and the electricians, wireless men and instrument experts certainly spared no efforts to keep the aircraft in tip-top condition.*

Actually this loco-busting is a most intriguing job. It is easier to find an engine when it has steam up and the results when it is wrecked are more spectacular — but of course we hunt out the stationary ones as well. Occasionally flying debris from them is hurled against the plane as it sweeps over immediately after the attack.

Flt. Sgt. Thorogood: *Yes, all sorts of amusing things happen. One of our pilots neatly shot the arm off a signal standard!*

Voice: How many locos does the squadron knock off in, say, a day?

Flt. Sgt. Thorogood: *Well, one day the squadron got as many as 19, and September was a record month, when 33 were destroyed or damaged.*

Voice: Yes. Your squadron certainly seems to be tearing up the Burma railway timetables. Here's wishing you good hunting and more power to your elbows — not forgetting the ground crews, of course. Well, cheerio Flight Sergeant, and thanks very much. Cheerio Flying Officer.

A further celebration followed the 100th locomotive destroyed when the whole squadron was on parade to witness the award, by no less a person than the Air Officer Commanding, of the DFM and the DFC to Sergeant Johnston and Flying Officer Dinwoodie for their recent action in destroying a large enemy oil storage tank (see photo).

Low level strafing sorties continued during September through to November-which brought about more casualties. FO Ball died of his wounds when he and FO Williams (pilot) attacked river craft at Yenanyaung. Sgt Humphries and Bainton were listed 'missing' when strafing a train at Toungoo, and FO Hassell and navigator Sgt. Thomas were shot down by enemy anti-aircraft fire while attacking targets in the Ywataung region.

Flt. Lt. Williams and his navigator FO Herbert had to crash land near Gyodaung, also Sgts Plummer and Collingwood were shot down near Thazi when they attacked four Japanese armoured cars. Their aircraft immediately burst into flames when they crashed.

Other casualties, happily not fatal, were the Beaufighters of Sgt Johnston DFM/FO Dinwoodie DFC, and Sgts Vincent/Mathewson. Both Beaufighters were severely damaged in sorties attacking motor convoys and Padaung, resulting in the crash landing of Sgt Johnson on return to base. Meanwhile, Sgt Vincent nursed his stricken aircraft back to base and made an excellent belly landing, having sustained severe damage to the rudder making it difficult to control.

On an operation in December the Beaufighters of Flt Lt Innes and WO Thorogood observed extensive defences were being constructed along the beaches of Ramree Island by the enemy, no doubt in anticipation of an Allied offensive. They were received hotly by the Japanese anti-aircraft units which caused damage to the hydraulics of Ron Thorogood's aircraft, resulting in making the undercarriage unserviceable. He immediately headed home for base overflying Agartala and making a first-rate belly landing at the nearby Maintenance Unit of Kanchrapara, for which he received a 'Green Endorsement'.

About this time momentous changes took place in the strategy of the war. South East Asia Command had been created at the Quebec Conference, and as a direct consequence the British and American Air Forces were combined to form a single fighting unit. Large consignments of latest marque Spitfires arrived at last to support 'the forgotten army'. The new Command was to have a new Supremo, Admiral the Lord Louis Mountbatten. As a destroyer captain at the commencement of the war he had had a meteoric rise to Chief of Combined Operations in Europe, having once nearly lost his life when his destroyer was sunk under him. The new

Combined Headquarters controlled the destinies of all the Royal Air Force operational units in North-East India and all those of the United States Tenth Army Air Force. Although complicated in lines of command, both British and American, it proved highly satisfactory in practice, the right and true spirit of co-operation prevailing.

The new command did not effect the function and organisation of No 27 Squadron and they continued their relentless operations against the Japanese with increased tenacity, 62 sorties being flown in the month of January, 1944. Wing Commander Nicolson was by this time well entrenched in the day-to-day organisation of ground and aircrew, and took an increasing participation in squadron operations, and leading by example. An idea of his role in the squadron is given by other members of aircrew.

Flt. Lt. Edgar Welch

James was with us a few months and never mentioned his previous career as a regular. His promotion had naturally been assisted by the privilege of his VC and I don't suppose that this made him popular with his seniors at Group etc. With us on the squadron he was always good company and entirely at home. I never heard him complain despite primitive conditions, the jungle — or bully beef ! He was a first-class experienced 'driver' of any plane and always patient with comparative beginners. I never saw him shoot in the air and do not know how effective he was. Ron Thorogood and I flew him down to Chittagong on occasions but only once went on operations with him — on the railway east of Mandalay, where Ron shot six locos. James proposed another trip to the same area with me as navigator, but Group vetoed this as interfering with their squadron programme.

I see from my log book that James' first monthly certificate of hours was October 1943, with an assessment for me 'above the average as an operational NAV/IN'. Remarks: 'Has completed a full operational tour with this unit, and has largely contributed to the magnificent success of his pilot during this time. Should prove most useful in any NAV/IN capacity, especially at low level work' (Signed) James B Nicolson VC, OC 27 Squadron.

Ron's log book was lost, but his assessment would have been similar. James recommended him for a commission, but was thwarted (by the Station Master, I believe). Ron did get the commission some months later.

From this you will gather that James was on good terms with the aircrews —especially the colonial's, who liked his style. He was fortunate in having the squadron delivered to him in good order, after the initial rough patch — with an excellent Engineer Officer in Mr Brewer, but a poor Adjutant. In all these words I'm just trying to paint a warm character, who was trying to achieve an assured place in a changing world. I cannot imagine what he would have made of the post-war years.

I see your photo of James with Leonard Cheshire, whom I knew briefly, but I doubt if they would have had much in common. Cheshire was Cheshire, with or without his VC, and did his best to demonstrate with dozens of operations that it is not what you do (or the numbers) but how you do it. I was introduced to him at Belvedere (when I was ADC to the Governor) and he borrowed an Anson. I do not know the purpose of his visit — there were only 96 bombers in Bengal at this time. In retrospect, we thought maybe something to do with his observation of the atom bomb on Japan — but actually he went westabout for that. The project for the dropping of the first bomb was not secret. The ADC to the Chinese General Cheu told me the week before (or maybe he was just fishing!).

Flt. Lt. R A (Paddy) Sterling

'My personal memory of James Nicolson is that he fitted completely the image of the typical Battle of Britain fighter pilot, gay, devil-may-care, excellent company, a natural leader and totally addicted to flying — particularly on operations. He loathed the safe desk jobs in which the RAF sought to keep him — possibly for the best of reasons — and it was with great delight and anticipation that he took over from Wing Commander Daish, who had set the pattern for the squadron before Nicolson arrived. We wondered how a single-engined fighter pilot would cope with the Beaufighter, which, apart from being twin-engined was also difficult to fly. It was fast for those days and the two powerful engines being set forward gave it a tendency to 'swing' on take-off, if not properly handled.

Again, the low level operations which were our main function in life meant that great skill and experience were required if crews were not to be lost unnecessarily. However, Nicolson took to it like a duck to water — apart from his initial reluctance to have a navigator in the aircraft; he maintained that he was a fighter pilot who had got about by himself until then and didn't see the need for a guide. However, the other pilots quickly disabused him and when he teamed up with Flt Lt Franklin they quickly became a very successful crew. I must say, in retrospect, that the character described by Dr Winfield in his book was not the one shown when he ran the day-to-day business of the squadron. As a Commanding Officer he was always approachable, gregarious, not too concerned about protocol and imbued with the objective of creating a unified and elitist group.

The only other occasion when our paths crossed was when I had my final crash on 2 May at Dum Dum airport, Calcutta. I was rushed to the military hospital in Calcutta and whilst in a semi-comatose condition was questioned by two RAF officers about what had happened to Nicolson, and where was he at the time of the crash? It was only later that I discovered that they had mistakenly supposed that I had been on the Liberator in which he was killed the same day. The fact that he was on the Liberator is typical of his reluctance to stick at a desk job and his addiction to operational flying.

Flt. Lt. A M (Alex) Dinwoodie DFC

'Two memories only remain of the CO. One is his waiting the arrival of our last 'op' — Sgt C Johnstone, was the pilot — and telling us that this would be our lot. Another excuse for a party of which I have very dim memories. But much more important, and still very vivid in my memory, and one which may throw another

shaft of light into Nicolson's character, was the one 'op' I did with him as his navigator. Not having my log book, I can't remember the target, but memory starts on leaving the Irrawaddy, to discover that the wireless set and the intercom were not working. I worked out the course for base, wrote it on a piece of paper, crawled up the belly of the Beau, and handed it to Nicolson. Back to the drawing board, and for the next half hour checked that we were on course. I worked out our ETA, another crawl and again handed it to the pilot. A few minutes before ETA I again joined him in the cockpit. By this time darkness had descended and to our horror there were no landing lights on. The next few minutes will always remain in my memory. I looked at Nicolson and his face was expressionless. A quick flick of the hands, an almost 'g' slip over the end of the runway, now barely visible in outline, and the sweetest landing I could ever remember. I draw a veil over subsequent events in the mess.

Although I am not sure, I believe Nicolson made familiarisation flights with others of the squadron navigators, which is a very fine trait in a Squadron Commander.'

In December 1943 the first of the de Havilland Mosquitos were taken on charge by the squadron, although they had been appearing in small numbers since April for a series of experimental trials, closely supervised by representatives of Rolls Royce and the de Havilland company. The Mosquito needed no justification for its presence in the squadron as it had earned itself a fine reputation in other theatres of war as an extremely fast and versatile aeroplane. In the role of photographic reconnaissance it was stripped of all defensive armament, relying on its fair turn of speed to outstrip any hostile enemy fighters. Being constructed of wood, and having glued joints, the 'wooden wonder' was very light and manoeuvrable, the twin-engines being the Rolls Royce Merlin.

On 16 December, Sqn. Ldr. Horn, 'A' Flight Commander, was given a special assignment, by flying, in a Mosquito, the Supremo, South East Asia Command, Lord Louis Mountbatten, on a tour of inspection of the Arakan front lines. They were accompanied by a fighter escort of Spitfires of No 615 Squadron.

Following a period of conversion, the first Mosquito operation was carried out on 21 December, when Wing Commander Nicolson and his regular navigator, Flt Lt Franklin, together with his No 2 — Flt Lt Thompson/Sgt Chippendale — attacked Japanese rolling stock and river craft in southern Burma. With the advent of Christmas, the usual tradition of the officers and NCO's to serve Christmas dinner on the other ranks was duly observed, but the merriment resulted in the Commanding Officer sustaining a broken wrist due to a 'fall'.

The New Year of 1944 saw a continuation of low-level sorties against enemy targets despite the poor weather, the operations being carried out by a mix of Beaufighters and Mosquitos, some of these at night. Since the operating range of the Mosquito was greater than the Beaufighter, this facilitated the attack of targets much further afield, the greatest distance example being one made by Flt Lt Torrance/Sgt Shortis on 13 January, when they strafed communications from Pegu, east of Rangoon, to Moulmein. This was a distance of 1200 miles from Cox's Bazaar, in the Arakan, the refuelling point out of Agartala.

On 7 January it was announced that Flt Lt Franklin (Frankie) the CO's popular navigator, had been awarded the DFC for meritorious service over the past months. The event was celebrated in fine style later in the mess.

On 7 February, 27 Squadron's personnel and equipment were moved yet again, this time to Parashuram, about 50 miles to the south of Agartala, and near to Fenny aerodrome, No 177's base.

On 9 March, No 27 Squadron flew its last Mosquito operational sortie, a general reconnaissance of Japanese aerodromes. Fine aircraft that it was, the Mosquito was not suited to the dank, humid, steamy conditions of Burma. Unlike the more sturdy robust Beaufighter, it could not take the heavy punishment meted out by the Japanese anti-aircraft batteries, and glued joints were affected by the hot climatic conditions. A recent statement by Ron Thorogood, who flew many missions with the 'Mossie', recalls that the engines were 'not as reliable as the radials of the Beaufighter, often returning from a sortie on one engine'.

Shortly after this final Mosquito operation, the squadron had cause for another celebration when the Beaufighter of PO Trudgeon beat up rolling stock and destroyed four locomotives, bringing the squadron total to 201. Sadly, PO Trudgeon and his navigator, FO Dobson were lost when their Beaufighter was hit by anti-aircraft fire south-east of Taungup. A further loss at this time was when the aircraft of FO Fairclough and Sgt Shaw failed to return from a jungle sortie. Yet another casualty was added to the squadron when Flt. Sgt. Skeen crashed on the airstrip when practising for the morrow's offensive sortie.

Under Nick's skilful, and almost obsessional stewardship, the squadron was further integrated into a fine fighting unit. No doubt, the ever-present conviction within himself that he had to prove his worthiness of the Victoria Cross inspired and drove him to the threshold of his physical and mental limitations. It is known that he was subject to recurring bouts of sickness and pain, the effects of his earlier severe burns in 1940, which had left him with a permanently clenched left hand. He led the squadron by example, taking on more flying duties than any other squadron member, and never asking a crew to execute a sortie that he was not prepared to undertake himself — rather the opposite — he tended to take on the more hazardous operations personally. The ground crews regarded him as a disciplinarian when it came to the maintenance and efficiency of the aircraft, in particular the engines which had to be capable at all times of flying the Beaufighter over the jungles of Burma, in the event of damage to either one.

Much of the operational successes that Nick enjoyed could be credited to the maturity and efficiency of his regular navigator — Flt Lt Franklin. The resultant combination of the two was a mix of skill, wisdom and initiative, and a common objectivity — to despatch the enemy as quickly and efficiently as possible.

The partnership was akin to a finely tuned clock — and having all the requisite compensations to attain optimum efficiency. Temperamentally they were at opposite ends of the pendulum, Franklin was older than his CO by several years, and in consequence had acquired a certain maturity and experience of life, whilst still retaining youthful courage and mental agility, quiet of nature and imperturbable. He was serious-minded, where Nick, by contrast, was ebullient, high spirited and sometimes explosive, if provoked.

An extract from the 3rd Tactical Air Force Public Relations department, written by one of their officers acting as observer with Nicolson and Franklin, gives a graphic description of an operational flight over enemy-occupied Burma.

'By the time we had reached the road running from Pauk to Pakokku in the lower Chindwin, we were flying at deck level and the pilot had to invariably 'lift' his aircraft to hop over trees. We soon spotted the first signs of life on that road —carts loaded with crates, probably carrying much-needed supplies for a Japanese unit. Our cannon made short work of them. I saw one cart disintegrate with the impact of our shells, whilst others were left in a cloud of smoke.

Then we found a convoy of seven carts. A single burst from a head-on attack caused complete havoc. One cart was broken up before the driver had a chance to avoid our fire. Others scattered madly down an embankment to overturn at the bottom.

We went on to the Irrawaddy where two large country craft were lying in mid-stream. They couldn't be missed. A sharp burst from our cannon riddled them amidships, leaving them slowly settling in the water.

Flying low, we saw a bunch of eight country craft — one of which blew up in a mass of black smoke and deep red flame after our attack. Others quickly caught fire. By the time we left they were all burning furiously.

As we swept past a high embankment we ran into a real hotbed of trouble. We were still skimming over the top of the river when a burst of 5 gunfire gave us the first indication that we had been spotted. In a twinkling, four or five different positions opened up with 20mm and 5 armament. In spite of our violent evasive action, AA fire came uncomfortably close, with shells plopping all around us. Flashes of red tracer bullets streaked above the cockpit and over both engines. At one time, it seemed as though our wing tips would hit the water in our effort to get away. Those Jap gunners were doing all they could to finish our patrol and they very nearly succeeded. But by skilful handling at such low level, the Wing Commander got us out of trouble. We speeded on to strafe sampans further up the river.

Back at base we found that the only damage sustained was a shell hole through the tail, and a few dents on the leading edges of the wings, where debris from a craft had struck as we pulled away from it. Our score for the morning was 27 river craft successfully attacked, apart from damage inflicted on supply wagons.'
API

On 25 March No 27 Squadron was ordered to move again, to Cholavarum, near Madras, and came under the aegis of No 225 Group. In April they were joined by No 47 Squadron, fresh from the Middle East. They were a torpedo-carrying Beaufighter squadron, and the two squadrons were to form a single unit operating against shipping in the Bay of Bengal, No 27's main function was to attack the enemy ship-born anti-aircraft batteries, whilst No 47 used their torpedoes. The result was that the 'Elephants' took over the major role of patrolling coastal waters.

The handicaps imposed by nature on the fighting men on the ground were to some degree burdensome to the airmen. To fly over the jungle was to traverse what seemed an endless green sea, which, although not a sea was devoid of landmarks as any stretch of ocean. Some sea and coastal patrols produced casualties caused by a phenomenon described by aircrews as 'a kind of mesmerism of water and mist' in which it proved almost impossible to distinguish between the surface of the water and the vaporous mists that poured down from the hills.

During the month of April one 'Beau' hit the sea when taking part in low-level practice, whilst another had to be ditched due to engine failure. The crew were picked up by local fishermen.

On 6 May 1944, Wing Commander Nicolson was relieved of his command of No 27 Squadron, and posted to 3rd Tactical Air Force Headquarters as Wing Commander Training. He was succeeded by Wing Commander J H McMichael. At this time, Nick was awarded the Distinguished Flying Cross for his fine work with the squadron, the citation read: *'Wing Commander Nicolson has consistently shown himself to be a courageous and enterprising leader. In spite of two spells of sickness caused by burns sustained in an action which gained him the Victoria Cross, he has always been eager to fly and lead his squadron personally on the most hazardous sorties. His fine example has been extremely valuable to the squadron.'*

This was a transitional period for the squadron. As well as a command change, new crews joined the unit not versed in operational flying, so for their benefit a comprehensive programme of training was instigated, involving formation flying, night and single engine flying, air-to-air and air to ground firing, and affiliation/ dinghy drill with Hurricane and Liberator aircraft.

The hard working Flt. Sgt. George Salter, 'B' flight's NCO Engineer, was awarded a much deserved British Empire Medal.

One of the original crews, PO Johnston DFM, and FO Alex Dinwoodie, DFC, was posted to No 21 Ferry Control at Karachi. FO Dinwoodie later joined the Special Low Attack Instruction School (SLAIS) at Ranchi as Chief Ground Instructor —and promoted to Squadron Leader. Another 27 Squadron officer, Flt. Lt. E B 'Bunny' Horn DSO, was also posted there as Chief Flying Instructor.

Flt Lt D J Innes, with his navigator, FO R A (Paddy) Sterling, had earlier been posted to No 2 Ferry Control, Allahabad, Central India, ferrying Beaufighters around India and Ceylon. They took up their new postings with some regrets, since they would rather have stayed on operations with the squadron. Since the formation of the squadron on 19 September 1942, they had been on continual operational flying and had flown 801 individual sorties, 32 aircrew had lost their lives on operations, three survived as prisoners-of-war and three were killed as a result of non-operational flying.

Flt Lt Franklin DFC, returned to England for a special navigation course —achieving 84.9%. He was tragically drowned later whilst swimming off Akyab (see Nick's letter to David Innes). WO Ron Thorogood and Flt. Sgt. Brian Harkness had been posted to Poona, near Bombay, as flying instructors. An all-night 'celebration' before they left for their new base did nothing to improve their condition for a long hot train journey.

It is not the purpose of this biography to enter into a detailed account of the war in Burma/India — fascinating though the prospect may be — but a summary of the situation at this time will suffice to illustrate briefly the fortunes of the conflict. In March 1944, the diversionary Japanese offensive known as the 2nd Arakan Campaign, was to commit large numbers of Allied troops in that theatre, whilst they applied their main effort on a major offensive southward into Bengal — the threshold of India. The Allies countered by their incredible, and magnificent, airborne offensive using the Douglas Dakota transport and gliders when 10,000 British troops complete with pack animals and equipment under the legendary Major General Orde Wingate, were dropped 150 miles inside the Japanese lines. The second, and major Japanese offensive in northern Burma was repulsed by the Allies after several months of intense fighting, aided in magnificent fashion by the superiority of the fighter air cover and the transport squadrons, who kept the lines of supply open against heavy odds.

The Japanese suffered heavy losses from the 8000 strong 50th Chinese Division under the command of the American, General Stilwell, who were transported, and supplied by air. They were active in the Assam region and recaptured airfields to be used once again by the Dakota squadrons for the widely dispersed supply lines. Following the fall of Kohima and Imphal, in the Chin Hills, in June 1944, the balance of power turned in favour of the Allies. The Japanese were constantly harried by the 11th Army under General Slim, and in the air the Hurri-bombers (converted Hurricanes), Spitfires, Vengeances and Thunderbolts created havoc for the retreating Japanese land forces.

Although No 27 Squadron was 'at rest' at Cholavarum, the Beaufighters of No 177 Squadron were engaged in long-range low level attacks on enemy communications in Central/Southern Burma. The Allied strategy was now to retake Mandalay and Rangoon, which they did on 21 March and 2 May respectively.

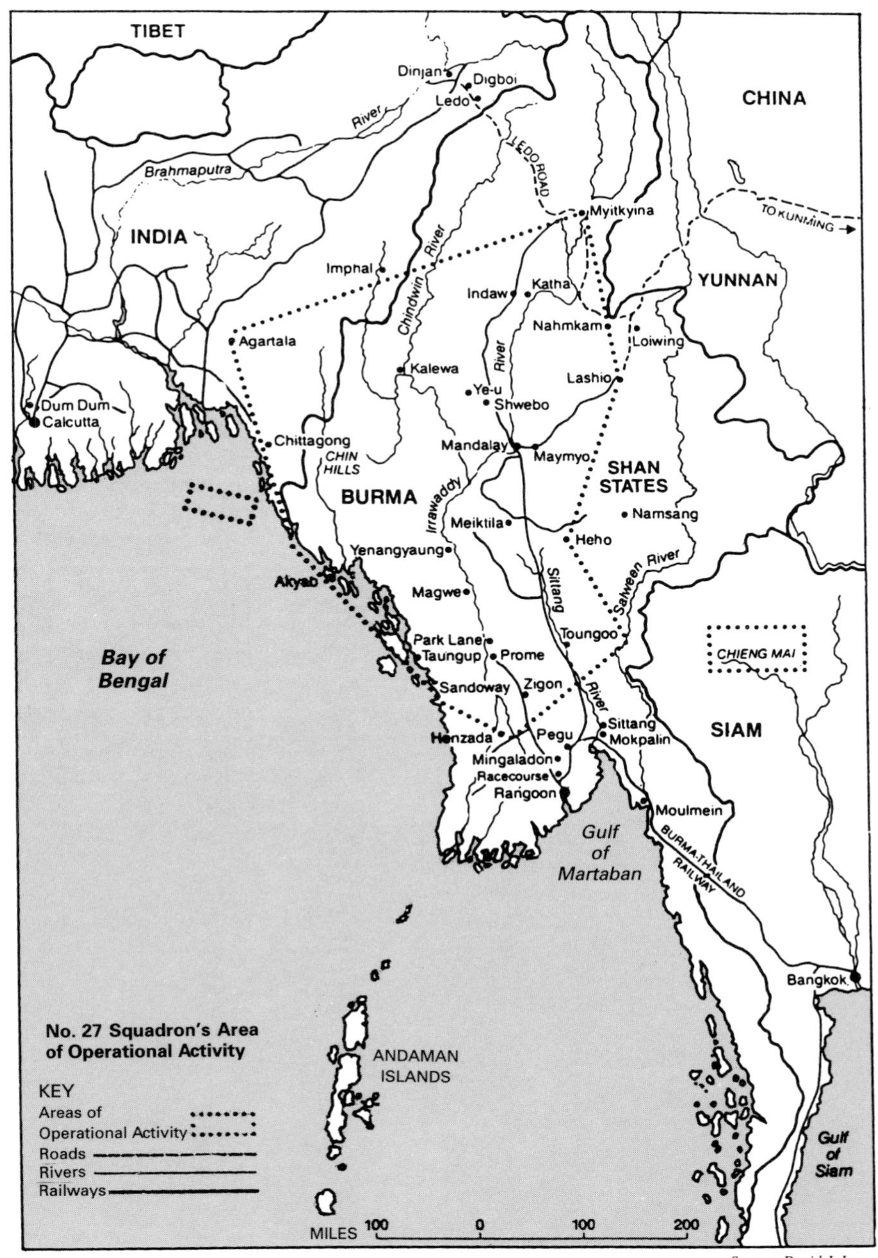

Source: David J. Innes

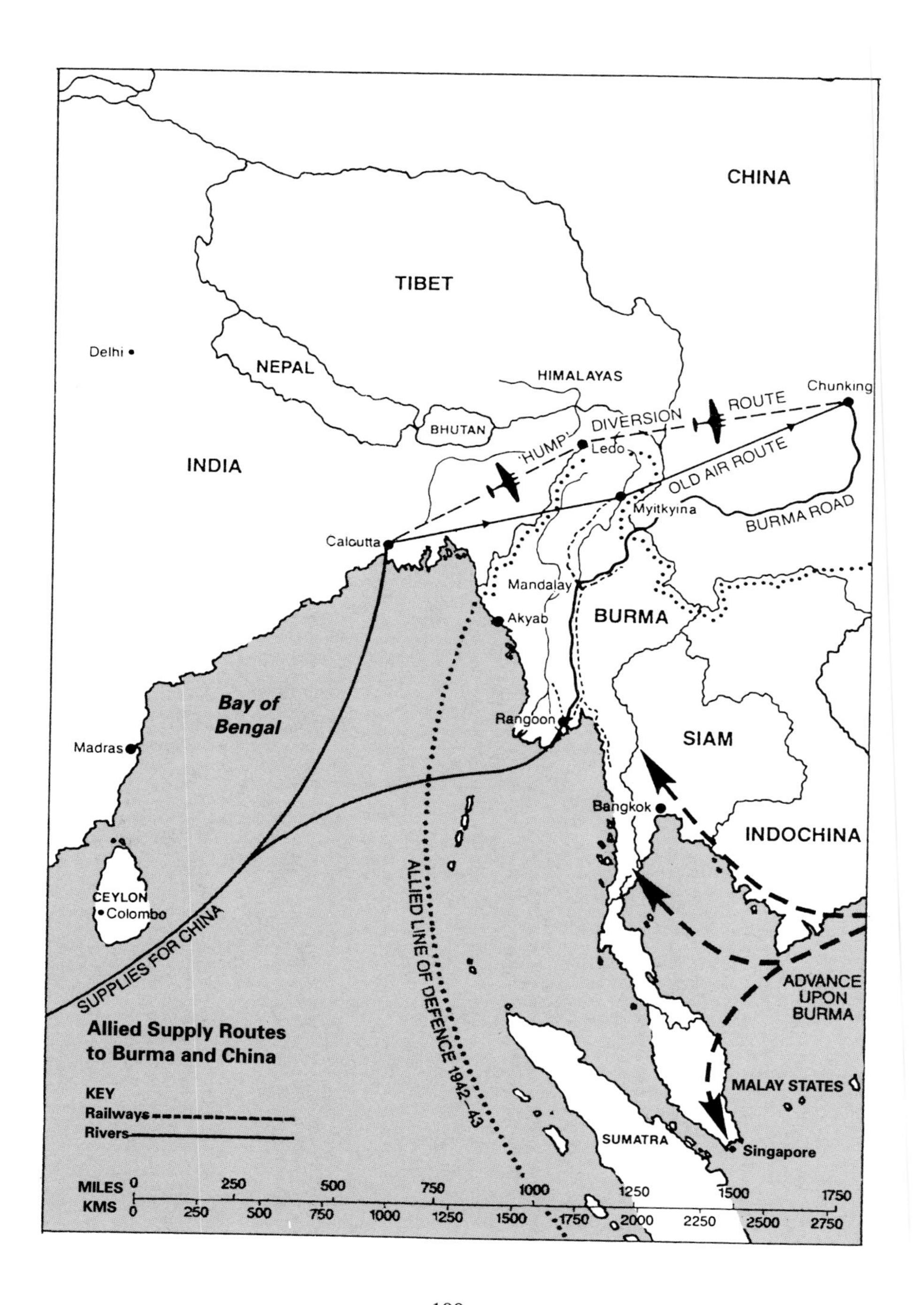

CHINA
TIBET
NEPAL
Delhi
HIMALAYAS
BHUTAN
INDIA
Chunking
'HUMP' DIVERSION ROUTE
Ledo
OLD AIR ROUTE
Myitkyina
BURMA ROAD
Calcutta
Mandalay
Akyab
BURMA
Bay of Bengal
Rangoon
Madras
SIAM
Bangkok
INDOCHINA
CEYLON
Colombo
SUPPLIES FOR CHINA
ALLIED LINE OF DEFENCE 1942–43
ADVANCE UPON BURMA
MALAY STATES
SUMATRA
Singapore
Allied Supply Routes to Burma and China
KEY
Railways
Rivers
MILES 0 250 500 750 1000 1250 1500 1750
KMS 0 250 500 750 1000 1250 1500 1750 2000 2250 2500 2750

Beaufighters of 27 Squadron in action in Burma

No 27 Squadron, Burma, 1943

Strike against Japanese targets — *Attack on Japanese storage tanks*

No 27 Squadron attacks Japanese locomotives

No. 27 Squadron concert party (Ain't Arf Hot Mum)

Mosquito in Burma

Source: Imperial War Museum

No 27 Squadron relaxing at base

No 27 Squadron soccer team.

Welch and Thorogood

Left to right
Nicolson, Marsland and Elsdon.

PO Johnson and FO Dinwoodie relaxing

Welch and Thorogood return from successful attack against Jap locomotives

Beaufighter crash landed at base after Jap sortie

Source: Imperial War Museum

Nick with Group Captain Cheshire at Viceregal party in Calcutta, 1944

Headquarters, formerly Palace of Maharajah of Cooch-Behar

Nick broadcasting on BBC. *Source: Imperial War Museum*

The Co's Navigator — F/L Franklin DFC.

Officers of No 27 Squadron 'on rest' at Cholavaram, Madras, in 1944

Source: Imperial War Museum

At Viceregal party, 1944, with General Auckinleck, Group Captain Cheshire and other VC's

Special low attack Instruction School, RAF Ranchi (India Command), July 1945
PO Chatterton, F/Lt Blakelay (IO), Capt Sharp (Army Liaison Officer), FO Calderwood, PO Adcroft, F/Lt Hope, S/Ldr Dinwoodie DFC (CCI), F/Lt Bollingbroke

The Duke of Gloucester, who visited an RAF fighter station in Bengal, about to shake hands with a sergeant pilot. On the extreme left is Wing-Commander Nicolson, the first fighter VC of the war, and third from left Air Vice-Marshal Stevenson, Air Officer Commanding

Telegrams :—"AIRVOICE." A. I. R. 1.

ALL INDIA RADIO,

CALCUTTA STATION.

TALKS BRANCH.

No. TE/W/456

To Date 19 .

22 OCT 1943

F/O E.Welch,
C/o Office of the A.D.P.R.,
7 Hare St., Calcutta.

DEAR SIR/MADAM,

We shall be pleased to broadcast your talk(s) on the subject, date, and time detailed below upon the conditions printed overleaf. We shall be obliged if you will kindly Sign and return the attached confirmation sheet, duly completed not later than the 22 OCT 1943 19 .

Title RAF Interview "Japanese detrained — The 100th Locomotive shot up in Burma.

Date(s) 22nd October, 1943 (E.R.)

Time of Broadcast As and when required

Duration 8 Minutes

Place of Broadcast Broadcasting House, Calcutta

Fee Honorary.

We would particularly ask you to assist us by complying with the condition that the manuscript of the talk should be in the hands of the Director not less than ten days before the date fixed for the broadcast. The normal routine of the station is seriously hampered if this condition is not observed.

Yours faithfully,

Msa.

Director.

For and on behalf of the Governor-General-in-Council.

Document for authorisation of radio talk, India, 1943

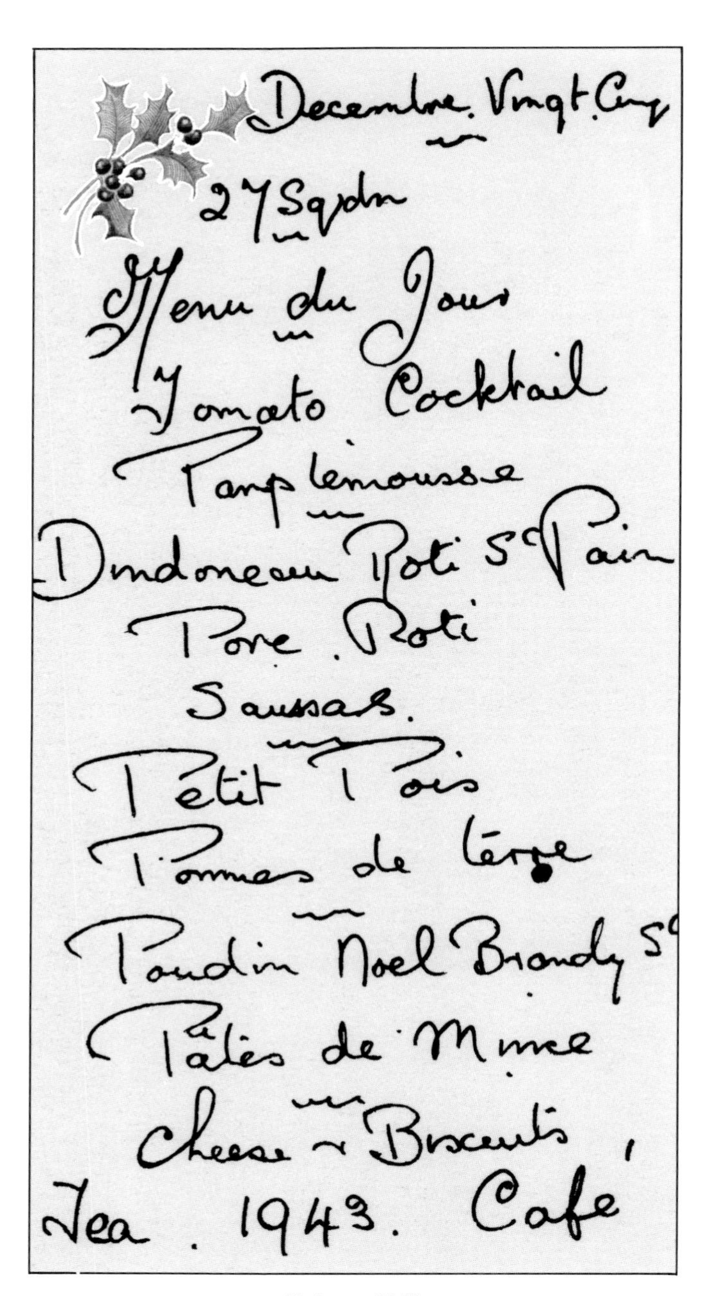
Decembre. Vingt Cinq

27 Sqdn

Menu du Jour

Tomato Cocktail

Pamplemousse

Dindoneau Roti Sc Pain

Porc. Roti

Saussage.

Petit Pois

Pommes de terre

Poudin Noel Brandy Sc

Pâtés de Mince

Cheese & Biscuits

Tea. 1943. Café

Christmas 1943.

Beaufighter of 27 Squadron.

Brian Harkness and Ron Thorogood relaxing in the local at Thirsk September 1990

CHAPTER 8

The last flight

In my beginning is my end
. . . in my end is my beginning.
East Coker (Four Quintets)
T S Elliot

On relinquishing the command of No 27 Squadron Nick proceeded to Headquarters, 3rd Tactical Air Force, Allied Command South East Asia, as supernumary —Training and Tactics. On 4 December 1944, he was again posted to Headquarters, Royal Air Force, Bengal/Burma with similar duties.

He took every opportunity to visit and participate in the activities of all the squadrons in his jurisdiction, and fly whenever possible with the crews on instructional exercises, which included No 355 (Liberator) Squadron based at Salbani, about 100 miles north-east of Calcutta.

Flt. Lt. Edgar Welch was a navigator and one of the original members of 'the Elephants', and when crewed up with WO Ron Thorogood made a very effective and successful team. Edgar left the squadron at Cholavarum in March 1944, and moved to various postings, one being the Aide to the Governor based at No 231 Group Headquarters, Belvedere. The building had formerly been the Palace of the Maharajah of Cooch-Behar and the residence of Lord Wavell. One day Lady Wavell called, and during a conversation with Edgar (now Squadron Leader) she mentioned that *'his office had some years ago been her bedroom when she was a young visitor!'*

His duties were mainly concerned with moving squadrons forward after each monsoon, and frequently met ex-squadron men passing through Calcutta, including 'Winco' Daish and James Nicolson. Towards the end of the war both he and Nick had the duty of assessing the roll of repatriated RAF prisoners recently released from Japanese prisons in the Rangoon area, and trying to establish who had 'made it' . On the evening of 30 April 1945, when he was about to close the office, Nick called in for a chat, and following this they walked across the botanical gardens and polo field to the big house serving as the officers mess. They passed an old man laid on a charpoy who had died earlier that day. His sons were taking him to the riverside for the ritual water ceremony at Khaliahat.

They had a pleasant evening and Edgar gave him a bottle of Worcester Sauce which Nick said was in short supply at Salbani. On parting, Nick went off into the dark to what Edgar presumed would be the Officers Club. There was a midnight curfew in Calcutta. Nothing was said about a proposed Liberator flight the next day.

Mr Frank Wootton was an Official War Artist with the Royal Air Force and had been seconded to No 355/356 Squadrons for duties at this time. On 1 May 1945 he was introduced to Nick by the Group Captain, who said that Nick had a 'watching brief' from the Air Ministry, and was to fly that night with the squadron, and 'would he look after Nick's collie dog whilst he was away?' Frank relates that many years later whilst having lunch at the formed HQ of Fighter Command, Bentley Priory, he was asked by the Commander in Chief, Air Marshal Hayr, if he would draw a portrait of James Nicolson for the Rotunda Room. The Rotunda contains many drawings made by Capt. Cuthbert Orde, an Official War Artist in 1940. There was no portrait of Nick, presumably he was in hospital at the time when the portraits were made. He was given a photograph of Nick and a painting was made, which now hangs among the other famous pilots of that era.

The purpose of Nick's assignment with 355 was to study monsoon weather conditions, identify the hazards, and to develop ideas to increase safety when flying in monsoon conditions. He also had a brief to advise on defensive measures from AA and enemy fighter attacks, and was always present at briefings — and debriefings. Although the nature and characteristics of monsoon weather was covered in great detail during operational training there was still much to learn. It was considered suicidal to fly through cumulo-nimbus cloud formations which had a cloudbase of some 500 feet rising to 35000 feet. The vertical currents within could be guaranteed to shake an aircraft to bits, presenting the Liberator pilots with the problem of fuel conservation, since the aircraft when laden had a practical ceiling of 27,000 feet and a cruising speed of 160 knots. Low flying meant more fuel consumed, and since the Liberators could not fly over the cumulus they had to literally fly above the waves so that they could smell the warmth from the sea. Those were the conditions.

Wing Commander Martin, the Station Commanding Officer, took the unusual step this day to inform all ground crew — flight mechanics, riggers and armourers — that they would be attacking Rangoon to soften up the enemy in preparation for the Allied invasion. In spite of the monsoon (as instructed by the C in C —Lord Louis Mountbatten) it would be an all-round-the-clock operation. It would be a case of take-off Salbani, target Rangoon and return to base, rearm, refuel and repeat the process. Since the flying time was of the order of eight to eight and a half hours return, this would involve three missions in the day.

Although Nick flew on Liberator KH.210 ('R' for Robert) he was originally detailed to 'crew up' on another aircraft as observer. The crew of this Liberator went to some trouble to fix up a desk in the aircraft to enable him to work, and were disappointed when he switched aircraft.

Liberator 'R for Robert' was captained by Wing Commander Gerald de Souza, a very experienced pilot, who had just returned from leave. He was the son of a very successful Indian businessman — the 'Oil King of India' — and educated at North Point, Darjeeling, which was run by Belgian Jesuits. In 1934 he studied in England as a Chartered Accountant, and on the outbreak of war he joined the RAF and trained as a pilot in Canada. The rest of the crew were also very experienced and this was to be their last sortie of the tour. The remainder of the crew were: WO Michael Pullen (second pilot), Flt Sgt Donald Cameron (engineer), PO Jack Spillard (navigator), Flt Sgt Eric Kightley, Sgts Robert Bell, Robert Helsby and FO John Calland (gunners), Flt Sgts Sam Doherty and Donald Nicolson (no relation) (wireless operators), and FO Brian Hill was the bomb aimer.

Liberator 'R for Robert' had already completed a round trip to Rangoon when Nick boarded for the second one of the day. At 0050 hours they again took off accompanied by seven other Liberators and set course for Rangoon, some 2000 miles away. At approximately 0250 hours came the first indication of trouble when the starboard outer engine burst into flame, followed shortly after by the starboard inner engine. Although the Liberator is capable of flying on two engines under normal conditions, with a bomb load of 6000 lbs — and in darkness — conditions were extremely hazardous, the aircraft tending to fly with one wing low.

Efforts were made to extinguish the fires but, in the event, were ineffective. Recognising the hopeless situation, Wing Commander de Souza jettisoned the bomb load and instructed the crew to prepare to ditch, in the well ordered, and well rehearsed manner. At 2.50 am approximately the Liberator struck the sea and sank within 15 seconds of impact. The second pilot, Michael Pullen and Gunner Eric Kightley, were catapulted through the perspex nose of the aircraft and landed in the water. Nick had been a model of calmness (according to Eric Kightley) and had asked to do whatever was necessary to avert the crash. Eric said that he gave him the thumbs-up sign before ditching and that was the last that he saw of him. The fact that the bomb doors were possibly still open would have accelerated the sinking of the Liberator and probably split the fuselage on impact, taking most of the crew with it. As it happened, there were four members of the crew in the water — Eric Kightley, Michael Pullen, Robert Helsby and James Nicolson. During a recent conversation, survivor Eric Kightley stated that the fourth person could have been Nick, but due to the darkness could not be sure. Eric had tried to inflate his life jacket but was unable to operate the inflation lever because of an injured wrist. He tried to inflate the jacket by means of the mouth tube but discovered that the bladder was ruptured. By a great stroke of luck he saw the nose wheel floating nearby and managed to tie his jacket tapes to it. He shouted to the other two men in the water that he had a nose wheel to hold on to, but Michael Pullen swam away and Robert Helsby was clinging to a box.

After 16 hours clinging to the nose wheel in shark-infested waters Eric Kightley had almost given up hope of rescue. Debris from the plane was floating over a wide area and the sharks seemed to be swimming closer — or was it just imagination ! Then it happened. The droning was getting nearer until finally he saw the Catalina circling overhead and it made a perfect landing on the water. The 'Mayday' distress call made by Flt Sgt Donald Nicolson had been received. The Catalina landed, almost drowning him when the float hit the nosewheel to which he was clinging.

One of the American crewmen hauled him aboard and made him comfortable. A second Catalina arrived and took aboard WO Pullen. He had suffered head injuries, bringing on hallucinations which accounted for his odd behaviour in the water. Sadly, no trace could be found of Helsby or any of the other members of crew.

Liberator 'R for Robert' had ditched about 300 miles from base, in an area known as the Sunderbunds, approaching the Mouths of the Ganges. Both survivors were taken to hospital in Calcutta, where they recovered from their ordeal, thankful that the hand of Providence had been kind to them. Mick Pullen died of a heart attack in 1972 whilst playing golf in Melbourne.

As to the root cause of the crash — the fire in the starboard Pratt and Whitney Wasp power unit — this would set up problems of stability and trim. When the second engine was engulfed with fire the situation would have been extremely hazardous, almost hopeless as far as control was concerned, which would account for the report of the aircraft flying one wing low. Since the Liberator had flown some 300 miles from base and attempted to return at the onset of the fire, relatively little of the fuel on board would have been used, offering little buoyancy from the tanks when the ditching occurred.

Although it was reported that the Liberators encountered less than normal enemy flak on their first bombing strike on Rangoon, there was always the chance that slight damage had been sustained to the engine, which had not been observed when they returned to base due to the speedy turn-around, in the darkness.

Officially, the engine fire and consequent failure was attributed to 'malfunction', but possible sabotage cannot be completely ruled out. Engine fire was an accepted operational hazard but could normally be extinguished with the built-in remedial systems.

Eric Kightley remembers that Nick had taken over the second pilot's position for a while, but later reverted to his observer's table when Second Pilot Mick Pullen assumed his normal role. Nick is reported to have asked if there was anything that he could do to help 'and I'll do it'. By this time anything that could be jettisoned to lighten the weight was thrown out . Eric recalls how matter of fact Nick was to the situation, his calmness no doubt influenced them all. He remained on flight deck whilst Eric took up his position in the rear — and with a 'thumbs-up' gesture from Nick, they parted.

On column 445 of the Kranji War Cemetery, which is part of the Singapore War Memorial, lies the commemoration to Wing Commander James Brindley Nicolson.

Also commemorated are the names of the crew of 'R for Robert' who were lost on 2 May 1945. The cemetery was started by Allied prisoners-of-war, but enlarged considerably in 1946 by the Army Graves Service, and adding graves from the notorious Japanese administered Changi Jail. Further graves were added by the Saigon Military Cemetery in French Indo-China and Bidadari Christian Cemetery in Singapore.

The Singapore War Memorial *Source: War Graves Commission*

Kranji Cemetery. Nicolson Commemorative Stone — with Franklin and de Souza

The ill-fated Liberator 'R for Robert'

The crew of Liberator ('R for Robert') relaxing

The Captain of Liberator 'R for Robert' Wing Commander de Souza

Muriel Nicolson and son James Gavin after being presented with Nick's DFC

CHAPTER 9

Brickbats and Bouquets

In the compilation of any serious biography, whether the subject be famous —or infamous, popular — or unpopular, it would not be responsible ere little point, if the biographer was not honest and objective. To produce hagiography for its own sake in deference to the subject, or any surviving relative, would be indefensible.

The fruits of material for this biography have emerged from several sources, be it the excellent — if somewhat protracted — service given by sundry archival institutions and museums, literary scribes, sometime acquaintances, or the phenomenally accurate, retentive memory of Muriel Nicolson, without whose support the work would not have been possible.

Inevitably, there will be those who will criticise, motivated by pathological dislike, or simply incompatability. Certainly James Nicolson's unorthodox manner and resistance to protocol did nothing to swell his reputation with some of his senior officers.

However, on balance, my accumulated viewpoint is that he has overridden these shortcomings, if considered as such, and his reputation has emerged unsullied. Certainly he had flaws in his character —who hasn't — but when taking into consideration the physical and mental tribulations consequent to his 'battle over Southampton' — and his silent, uncomplaining acceptance of his undoubted injuries —he has my unstinted admiration, and is fully entitled to a measure of unorthodox, perhaps maverick behaviour.

The following unadulterated narratives give a further dimension to his character, and influence on others.

Wing Commander Roland Winfield DFC AFC

Roland Winfield joined the RAF in 1939 as a medical officer, and later qualified as a pilot, taking a particular interest in the problems encountered by flying personnel, and was later appointed chief assistant to the RAF Consultant in Applied Physiology, Royal Aircraft Establishment, Farnborough.

He specialised in medical research into airsickness, the effect of extreme cold, fatigue, sleep, wakefulness, oxygen starvation, searchlight dazzle, flying clothing, dinghies, seat harness, crash stations and injuries to parachutists. He took an active part in experimental exercises, sometimes hazardous and of unknown consequences. He accompanied Prime Minister Winston Churchill on many of his visits to overseas conferences, and took part in many operational tours for which he was awarded the AFC in 1942 and the DFC in 1944, and was allotted the rare privilege of the use of his own aircraft. In December 1943 he was sent by the Air Ministry on a fact-finding tour of the South East Asia Command, arriving at Agartala on New Year's Day 1944, when he commenced what transpired to be a close working relationship with Nick. They flew operational sorties together over enemy occupied jungle, accompanied by navigator, Flt Lt Franklin. He recorded his admiration for Nick in moulding the squadron into the finest instrument of war that he had come across in India, and the way that he had done it.

He had inspired a loyalty within the squadron by the excellent example that he set —the highest form of loyalty born of discipline and leadership. By choosing the most hazardous strikes himself, and by flying more operations than anyone else, he promoted a spirit of confidence unique in his experience in India and commanded its spirit of complete operational efficiency.

Dr Winfield records that *'Nicolson was haunted by the doubt of whether or not he was really worthy of the VC that he had won. He confided that he would never know if he would have done what he did had he had the time to weigh up the pros and cons in cold blood. If you're given a decoration that you can't refuse, and yet you are not sure that you deserve it, then you have to shape your life, or what's left of it, in an honest attempt to show yourself and the rest of the RAF that at least you have tried to earn it. To my mind, there is not a shadow of doubt that he was worthy of his Victoria Cross, and probably deserved a Bar to it for the manner that he commanded 27 Squadron. This is one of my most firmly held beliefs.*

Nicolson, and his navigating officer, Franklin, made up a crew of a Beaufighter, the combination of which was a mix of initiative, skill and wisdom that formed the most formidable crew I ever flew with.'

Wing Commander Tom Neil DFC AFC AE RAF(Retd) (ex 249 Squadron)

The last time that I had seen Nick was at Boscombe Down in 1940. My next meeting with him was in India in March 1945 when I was en route to Burma — Nick was then a Wing Commander staff officer at Eastern Air Command, mixed British and American formation located near Calcutta. On that occasion he greeted me rapturously as a long-lost brother, telling everyone the most enormous fibs about my prowess as a fighter pilot, so convincingly, in fact, that I really began to think that he was believing his own stories — Nick always had a lively imagination.

After several days and nights of hard partying together, during which his good spirits, anecdotes and mimicry particularly relating to his American colleagues were quite memorable, I moved to Burma, only to learn later that he had been killed taking an unauthorised flight in a Liberator.

Marshal of the RAF, Sir John Grandy, GCB GCVO KBE DSO (ex Commanding Officer 249 Squadron)

I have the greatest admiration for Nick, his guts, his determination, and all he achieved. We first met when, with 20-odd others, he came under my command on the formation of 249 Squadron in May 1940. In August, only three extremely busy months later, he was shot down. I saw Nick but once again after we took off that day; this was a chance and momentary meeting somewhere in Burma in 1945, some 45 years ago.

Sqn Ldr P H V Wells DFC RAF(Retd) (ex 249 Squadron)

I arrived on posting to RAF Leconfield from No 5 OTU in June 1940, and soloed on a Hurricane the next day. I think that Nick showed me the cockpit etc, but I see that 'Boozy' Kellett signed my log book as Officer Commanding, 'A' Flight. On 8 July we moved to Church Fenton and for a month I see that my log book is signed by Nick, who spent a great deal of time training us in formation flying, fighter attacks etc. He was exceedingly patient and thorough in all this. However, I do remember complaining bitterly at having to do stall turns in formation with him at around 500 feet. To give him his due he never made me do it again. Nick was comparatively recently married so we did not see much of him in the mess in the evenings because he lived out. He was always impatient for us to move south — and get into the action. We left Church Fenton for Boscombe Down on 14 August 1940, and of course you know the rest of the story.

Wing Commander R A Barton DFC RAF (ex 249 Squadron)

Both Nick and I were posted to No 249 Squadron at Church Fenton about mid-May 1940, to reform under the command of Squadron Ldr John Grandy. I was given the command of 'A' Flight and Nick was my most senior and experienced fighter pilot, the rest of the flight being war-entry.

On 16 August 1940, whilst based at Boscombe Down, the six Hurricanes of 'A' Flight were ordered to investigate reported enemy raiders in our vicinity. During the flight Nick reported sighting enemy aircraft, which I failed to see, so I ordered his section of three aircraft to reconnoitre the situation. The Hun aircraft were some distance away, and as it happened were engaged by Spitfires and shot down. When returning to rejoin the main flight his section was bounced by the enemy, which really maddened Nick, prompting the action which he took against the Hun aircraft.

Later, Nick returned to the squadron when the unit had moved from Boscombe Down to North Weald. He was convalescing from his wounds and burns, but was not fit for flying and was duly posted away. This was the last time that I saw him.

Flt Lt David J Innes RAAF(Retd)

David Innes, Royal Australian Air Force, served with No 27 Squadron in Burma under Wing Commander Nicolson, and wrote a splendid book on the subject entitled 'Beaufighters over Burma' which the writer has used for references. In late 1944 he was repatriated to Australia, and it was from there that he sent a newspaper cutting to Nicolson drawing his attention to an article where his name had been included in a list of Australian airmen who had been successful in aerial operations in South East Asia in 1944.

Nick replied to the 'announcement' by writing to the newspaper office as follows:

Dear Sir,

In a cutting from a copy of your worthy daily (undated) I was amazed to learn that I am an Australian; a fact that had hitherto been kept secret from me. The cutting was forwarded to me by Flt Lt D J Innes who served with me in Beaufighters in 1943 and 1944.

I regard my adoption and consequent conversion to an Aussie from a Pommie in a very favourable light and particularly for the following reasons:

(a) I'm now owed a large sum of money at RAAF rates for my overseas (tax free)

(b) I should be eligible for Australian amenities! (plum cake please)

(c) I'm due for repat to NSW at any moment (and some beer!)

My very kind regards to you, and your staff, and best wishes for 1945 to all of you down under.

Yours sincerely,

James B Nicolson RAAF (late RAF)

The following letter was written by Nick to David Innes from HQ RAF Bengal/Burma, RAF India, 25 January 1945 (the original is deposited in the archives of the RAF Museum, Hendon).

My dear Dave,

I just received your letter dated 8 January — and l am still licking my chops at the thought of all that beer!

I've tried to get Peter Thompson a flight with Paddy Sterling[1] *as his navigator, but don't know if it has come off yet, they're both very keen, anyway. I enclose a short letter to the editor of your daily, which you might forward to him after reading.*

I couldn't send it direct as I don't know the name of the paper or the Editor's address for readers' letters.

I am very surprised to learn after all these years that I am after all, an Aussie despite what my parents told me. There's justice for you and to think that after all these years I am a citizen of the 49th state! It just goes to show doesn't it; my father must have had a bycicle (bicycle ? yes) after all ! Sorry about the spelling bi-what

[1]Paddy Sterling — David Innes regular navigator.

not wrong first time but the 'y' got out of hand and wanted to be nearer the front. Trig's show was indeed a tragedy and I had some very hot words with the General himself, and won in the end [2] *He was avenged the other night when we pulled down one of their big jobs by mistake.*

I had a Christmas card from Snowy in Bombay, don't know where he is at the moment. He's due back home anyway, so was probably on the boat when he sent it.

'B' 16[3] *went home before you and I believe Clegg's on the way too.*

Managed to get Bill House back among the boys as John Cotter's navigator, and they are both pleased with life. I wouldn't give up hope about something coming your way eventually. I did my best for you and Paddy. You're not supposed to know, but what the hell ! You haven't got a Beaufighter squadron lying around without a CO have you ? You might remember that I'm fed up with my chair (non-swivel variety) in 'Fort Confusion' and would like to get up to 50 again myself sometime.

Nicholls is still going strong, but I'm afraid Chalky had it about two ?? ago. At night. The war is indeed going well for once, and the local army has its finger well out.

I've volunteered for another year out here to see the clean-up. Frankie[4] *got 84.9% on his staff nav. course, and when I last heard of him he was on two months quasi-leave (supposed to be duty) at home. He should be back with us in the near future. One or two stories for you. Two English girls talking in a bedroom and one says: 'Damn bad luck, poor old Bob, four years in India and he breaks his leg running upstairs.' And the other one about the superstitious rabbit who left his burrow to go to the local one evening and seeing the new moon went back to his burrow and turned over his doe!*

My regards to any of the boys you come across on your little island (or should I say OUR little island ?) and if you get a Beau back under your bottom you might also come across our Charlie Crombie.

Have six or seven pints for me sometime when you're feeling thirsty and good luck for 1945. Keep yourself in one piece and remember Isaac Newton's 11th Law of 'gravity' — no matter how you shake it the last drip always goes down the trouser leg.

Enough of this, I must do some work (yeah?). Drop me a line again when you're not too busy. God bless.

Yours eye,

Nick

[2]PO E W M Trigwell, an Australian pilot of No 27 Squadron, with his navigator, PO Chippendale, in November 1944, were briefed to attack road transport on the Taungup Pass, when without warning, their Beaufighter was attacked by two USAAF Lockheed P.38 Lightnings. Their aircraft and another Beaufighter of the same flight, were both shot down. Trigwell was able to crash land his aircraft in about four feet of water, and although he was not injured, his navigator 'Chips' was badly wounded in the back by cannon shells and was unable to move. Triggy managed, with difficulty, to pull Chips out of the wrecked aircraft and bandage his eight wounds with torn-up strips of parachute. After four days Chips died and Triggy was taken prisoner by the Japanese, and suffered ill-treatment in their hands. He was eventually repatriated to Australia

[3]Squadron Leader Bassingthwaite — so called B16 universally for ease of use.

[4]Flt Lt Franklin — Nicolson's regular navigator.

The Story of a Street Name

Have you ever considered how a road gets its name? When a developer puts up a street of houses or a new estate, he consults with the District Council for suitable names for these roads. The Local Authority usually has a few thoughts that are associated with the locality, requests may be received from various outside sources, and the developer himself may have some ideas of his own. As far as possible the duplication of like-sounding names to existing roads in the area is avoided and here the advice of the Post Office is sought — nothing is more irritating than having your mail regularly delivered to the wrong house in a similarly named road to your own.

In the late 1960s a suggestion had been made to the then Shoreham-by-Sea Urban District Council that perhaps a development could be named in honour of the late Wing Commander James Brindley Nicolson VC DFC. At the Council's Planning and Building Committee meeting of 29 September 1969 this suggestion was considered in relation to naming the new spine road of the Buckingham Nurseries development, after Wing Commander Nicolson. This was approved wholeheartedly —Nicolson Drive was born.

For some unaccountable reason when the street nameplate was manufactured the Nicolson became Nicholson. Even after the nameplate was erected there was no apparent query on the spelling and the Council's own archives had failed to reveal any more about the error.

So the incorrect name became established — it even found its way onto the Ordnance Survey map for the area. The red faces were to come many years later.

In the early 1980s a resident of Nicolson Drive wrote to the Council querying the spelling of their road name. The District Council's Planning Officer indicated his willingness to put the matter before the Councillors for their next consideration provided the person who originally wrote in would provide the full support of all the neighbours. This was never forthcoming, so the matter was left in abeyance.

In May 1986, the Honorary Secretary of the Shoreham-by-Sea Branch of the Royal Forces Association, Mrs Angela Riley, wrote to ask if the correct spelling could be provided. At this stage it was felt by the officers and members of the Council that this error could no longer remain unaltered.

Now to change the name of an existing road, albeit only to alter the spelling, is more complicated than providing it in the first place. Many people have to be approached to see if there are any objections to such a name change. For example, all the statutory bodies, the emergency services, the Post Office, and of course the people most affected, the local residents themselves. Not surprisingly, because of the reason for this name change, no objections were received.

And so, Nicholson Drive became Nicolson Drive to re-establish Shoreham's own tribute to their brave local war hero.

(The above material was kindly provided by the Adur District Council.)

Local Commemoration

To commemorate the 30th anniversary of the parachute descent and landing of Flt Lt. James Nicolson on 16 August 1940 following his epic dog-fight with enemy fighter aircraft over Southampton, Mullards (now Philips components) erected a memorial on, or near, the location where he landed. This area is now an industrial estate but at the time of Nick's landing was an open field owned by Mr Strange, at Burrowdale Road, Millbrook.

The memorial was unveiled by Mrs Muriel Nicolson on Sunday 16 August 1970, and among those present was Mr Eric Coleman, who was a Police Constable at the time and was on hand to attend to Nick, who was in a very serious condition due to wounds and extensive burns. He took down the message for the telegram which was sent to Muriel from the local Post Office at Redbridge. Also present at the ceremony were two other men who went to Nick's aid — Mr F Lisle and Mr E A Dukes.

Commemoration at RAF Boscombe Down

In order to remember Flt Lt Nicolson's act of heroism on 16 August 1940, his former operational base at the time of the action, Boscombe Down, has erected a memorial in his honour. The memorial takes the form of a stone plinth engraved with a simple inscription relating to the action.

RAF Brize Norton Memorial Aircraft

No 10 Squadron has on charge eleven VC.10 aircraft all of which carry the names of Victoria Cross winners. Aircraft number XV.107 carries the name of James Nicolson in his honour.

Wing Commander H J S Beazley DFC RAF (ex 249 Squadron)

I was not in Nick's flight ('A' Flight, I believe) and by the nature of things was not nearly so well acquainted with him as those who were. However, I still retain a very clear recollection of him as a cheerful and enthusiastic extrovert. Like a number of others in the squadron I came direct from Cranwell FTS and the University Air Squadron. We were a very happy bunch, and the thing that impressed us was the complete absence of 'bullshit' and the friendly reception given to us by the 'Regulars', and the Flight Commanders — of which Nick was one. My first main recollection of him was when he took me up in a Miles Master, after I had put up a rather dismal first 20 minutes or so with someone else. His infectious good nature immediately made me feel that I could cope, and my log book shows that 30 minutes later I was happily flying a Spitfire for the first time, having previously been flying the dear old Hart variants. Later we all went to Acklington for air-firing practice, and for some reason he took three of us on an Indian file tail chase at low level, doing his best to shake us off. One member came back declaring him to be a mad b - - - and that he had nearly hit a tree! But, in fact, it was great fun, a good test of flying, and it did much to inoculate us with the conviction that fighters were meant to be thrown about — and no occupation for the staid!

Nick was always telling us stories of flying in tight formation and having his wing tip gently tipped up by the chap next to him. I still believe his stories were true. He truly believed that the only life worth living was that of a fighter pilot and nobody could be in his company for long without being convinced of this also —always supposing that they needed convincing.

When the squadron moved south to Boscombe Down, Nick was in his element and raring to go. He was most displeased when it became known that 'Butch' Barton had made the first major contact with the Hun.

We didn't seem to have much social life, as you can well imagine, but I seem to remember coming to the mess when we were at Church Fenton, and we had a most cheerful party, with an almost peacetime atmosphere. Again, I think we were all pleased in having John Grandy as our Squadron Commander, and Nick and Butch as our two Flight Commanders.

Eventually we both met again at the Palace Hotel hospital, and I well remember the night that news of his Victoria Cross award came through. He seemed slightly dazed by it all, but I don't think it went to his head in the slightest degree, and he remained the same cheerful extrovert with not an ounce of side in his nature.

PO R W 'Wally' Wallens (later Wing Commander R W Wallens DFC)

'My recollection of Nick was a brief and unplanned meeting at RAF Church Fenton in April 1939. At this time I was under training with No 41 Squadron at Catterick and was, with others, detailed for a cross-country night flight from base to Digby in Lincolnshire, to refuel and return. The Met. Office had forecast good visibility and fair conditions. At 3000 feet I set course for Digby, the landmarks on my track coming up well . . . the lights of Northallerton, Thirsk and York, and the Rivers Ouse and Trent gleaming in the moonlight. Over Doncaster the weather suddenly deteriorated and heavy cloud formations started to build up, and losing height to avoid them, heavy rain beat on the windscreen and canopy, visibility worsening by the minute. I had switched radio channels and called Digby control but after several calls static background noise obliterated everything and eliminated all chance of contact.

I realised that I was not going to get in to Digby that night and set a reciprocal course for Catterick, hoping that the weather had not closed down there as rapidly as it had here. I was blissfully unaware that a recall had gone out from Catterick as the storms moved in eastwards over the Pennines with unexpected speed, as I had been beyond radio range. Now flying in very heavy rain just below cloud base, and fervently hoping for an improvement in the weather, it was painfully obvious that I was in the middle of a particularly unpleasant frontal system. Having of necessity dropped altitude to 300 feet and with canopy open and landing light on, passed over what I appraised to be Goole, and the Hull-Selby railway line flashed by quickly. I weighed up my chances of getting back to Catterick in such conditions as very slim. Staying low, the railway lines led me to Selby and over the small old airfield of Sherburn in Elmet, and swinging very hard right I knew the line north to York would in a few moments direct me to the verge of the airfield boundary of RAF Church Fenton. As I kept the line on my left the western boundary flashed by under my starboard wing. In the lashing rain I swung hard right and left again into a tight circuit of the airfield, ominously dark with only the lights of the messes and quarters, blinking below. I couldn't help grinning to myself, imagining the look on the faces as I roared over the roofs, and their indignation at being so rudely disturbed over their ale — and how I could do with one just now! I circled very low, flashing Morse signals on my downward recognition light, with touching pleas for a flare path, but no-one seemed particularly interested in my plight. I waited with restrained impatience for someone to lay on a few flares and a floodlight, until, prompted to check my instruments I realised how low my fuel was running, and emptying fast.

Lights were now flickering around the Watch Office and I felt sorry for the men who had been pressed into action to help me in the torrential rain, but I could wait no longer, and, dropping my undercarriage, did a slow run down hoping they would get the message that I was coming in, regardless.

Landing a Spitfire at night with the existent facilities of base was no easy matter and to attempt it with no aids, in low clouds and heavy rain conditions, on a strange airfield presented problems I must now resolve. The first attempt must be the only one, with everything right in the way of approach, despite the strong westerly wind. I came downwind just outside the south boundary, lowering my undercarriage and tightening my harness until it hurt offering up a quick prayer before throttling back and quickly flipping the flaps selector to 'Down'. I was committed — and decided that I must overshoot slightly and side-slip in for better visibility and jammed on right rudder regardless, feeling the wind and rain blinding in to the port side of the open canopy. I kicked hard left rudder until the aircraft swung straight and lined up for touch down. The grass surface was a wet dark blur and I couldn't judge my height and had a terrible feeling that the aircraft would drop from my hands. A quick burst of throttle and I caught it as it settled and before I knew it the Spitfire had put me down with hardly a bump and rolled up the airfield in total darkness.

I felt the tension drain away as I taxied up to the welcoming lights of the Watch Office, braked and switched off the engine — sitting in silent gratitude for a moment. I removed my soaked leather helmet and oxygen mask, climbed from the cockpit and closed the canopy, thinking 'If the bar's closed I shall go bloody mad!'. Making my way to the Mess, which thankfully was still open, I proceeded to 'sink' a fair quantity of the local brew. Among the motley aircrew partaking there was a tall, loquacious Pilot Officer who introduced himself as James Nicolson. I recall quite clearly, as I leaned against the mantle-piece he made some funny 'crack' about my disturbing the peace, which at that precise moment did not amuse, but which we agreed, after a few more beers, was most appropriate. It transpired that the unexpected storm that evening played havoc with other night flying exercises in the region and one or two aircraft were lost and pilots missing, with several others crashing on landing in the foul weather.

I flew back to Catterick the following morning and was told to report to the CO's office, where he sat with my Flight Commander. He told me that they managed to recall all the aircraft behind me but I was out of range. Digby had heard my first call but couldn't make contact. They thought that I was lost until the message came through that I had landed at Church Fenton. The CO added: 'to land a Spitfire at night on a strange unlit airfield in storm conditions is no mean feat. I am very proud of you and pleased that you are with 41 Squadron'.

Group Captain T A F Elsdon OBE DFC RAF (Retd)

James Nicolson and I served together with No. 72(F) Squadron at Church Fenton and I recall that he was a very good pilot — good enough to be selected with 'Elmer' Boulter (a Belgian) to carry out the synchronised aerobatic display for Empire Air Day in 1939. We had kept three Gladiators on strength for this occasion when the squadron was re-equipped with Spitfires, two in 'A' Flight for Elmer and Nick, and the other for myself attached to 'B' Flight to carry out the individual aerobatics. Unfortunately, the final inspection before the display revealed that one of the main longerons on one of the 'A' Flight Gladiators had sheared, consequently the performance as far as 'A' Flight was concerned had to be cancelled. I was more fortunate in 'B' Flight.

Nick was an incredibly accurate snooker player, adept at potting the balls hard and with demon precision, particularly after dinner in the evening.

We were both posted later to the Far East serving in the same theatre I was initially Wing Commander Flying 293, whilst Nick commanded No. 293 Wing at Alipore (my term there being October 1942 to January 1943). Shortly afterwards our roles were reversed when I went up to command No. 169 Wing at Agartala —a Mohawk Wing — and Nick joined my Wing as Officer Commanding No. 27 Squadron, a Beaufighter squadron known as the 'Flying Elephants', recently reformed into a very effective offensive unit. He stayed with the squadron for about twelve months leaving in June 1944. I departed from 169 Wing in October 1943 deployed as commander of one of the forward fighter Wings.

Perhaps on a more domestic note, and which may be of interest to your readers is the story of two Himalayan bears. In 136 Squadron (the Woodpeckers) we had a baby bear which was adopted as a pet by one of the squadron members, which naturally grew, and grew, until it ceased to be a pet but became a public menace —particularly when it crashed into a crate of very precious eggs, demolishing the whole consignment. It was then that Warrant Officer Mangan made the bear understand that he was socially undesirable and promptly made a hasty exit into the jungle — not to be seen again.

When No. 27 Squadron joined me in 169 Wing later, I was more than a little apprehensive to discover that they had arrived at Agartala complete with their own pet bear and at four feet tall, almost full grown. He too soon became a social problem, but unlike bear No. one he could not be persuaded to seek a more normal habitat for himself in the jungle. Finally Nick came up with a very expedient, humane, perhaps unorthodox solution for all concerned. He arranged for a parachute harness to be suitably modified to fit the proportions of the bear's torso, and for it to be dropped by parachute into a clearing in the jungle —some way from Agartala.

I was assured that the parachute opened perfectly and the bear was last seen dropping toward some small trees, and I have no doubt that, intelligent as he was, had no difficulty in disengaging himself with his sharp teeth from the harness —after landing. I have no doubts that the bear soon adapted to his new and more natural environment in the jungle.

Perhaps we should be thankful that the squadron refrained from following the depiction of the squadron crest — and refrained from adopting an elephant!

T A F Elsdon

(Author's note: It is with great regret that I record the death of Group Captain Elsdon's son who was Officer Commanding No. 27 Squadron in the recent Gulf conflict and was killed in action in that theatre.)

'How quickly passeth the glory of this world'

Thomas a Kempis

Muriel Nicolson was informed of her missing husband by telegram on the last day of the War in Europe, 2 May 1945. On 29 October she was presented at an investiture in Buckingham Palace with her husband's posthumous award of the Distinguished Flying Cross. She was accompanied by her five-year-old son, James Gavin.

For many years Muriel lived in the country cottage in Kirkby Wharfe that she shared with her husband, and then moved on to 'Greatwood', a charming, secluded cottage not far from Tadcaster. She never remarried after her tragic loss, but devoted herself to the upbringing of her young son, on a war widow's pension — an almost impossible task which meant foregoing most of life's luxuries and being forced to accept a standard of living far below that which relates to the widow of a serving officer who had paid the price with his life.

She nursed both of her parents through terminal illnesses, and a sister who suffered for many years the ravages of cancer.

Since 1945 Muriel had been an ardent campaigner for the case of the deprived war widow, and in order to focus their plight to the nation, and beyond, she decided to auction her husband's Victoria Cross and other war medals, along with personal artefacts. Nick's tattered and burned uniform was gifted to the Tangmere Military Aviation Museum on loan in perpetuity, where it can be seen in its humidity controlled glass casing. The Victoria Cross and other medals brought a record sum of £110,000, paid for by public funds and bought by the Trustees of the Royal Air Force Museum, Hendon. The effects of the auction under Lot 19 were sold by Messrs Glendinning & Co, under the description of the following:

(a) Photocopy of Wing Commander Nicolson's Flying Log Book

(b) The flying jacket he was wearing during the action leading to the award of Victoria Cross

(c) Telegram from the Air Ministry informing him that he is to receive the VC from HM King George at Buckingham Palace

(d) Telegram of congratulation from HQ No 11 Group

(e) Medical Certificate dated 17/11/40 granting 21 days sick leave

(f) Numerous photographs — with the original ribbon bar with VC (no emblem) and the 1939-45 Star ribbons

On her late husband's birthday, 29 April 1985, Muriel suffered a devastating personal blow when her only child, James Gavin, was killed in a road accident at Boroughbridge, in Yorkshire. Gavin had been educated at Rugby School with a bursary awarded by the Royal Air Force, progressing to Oxford as a Kitchener Scholar. He was 44 years of age when he died, and had married but the union was broken through incompatability. There were no children — and no-one to perpetuate the family name.

In December 1988, Muriel suffered a further grievous loss when her great friend and companion, Brigadier Stuart Knox CBE, died at Greatwood after a short illness.

DAILY NEWSPAPER OF SOUTH EAST ASIA COMMAND

STATESMAN HOUSE
CALCUTTA

27th May 1945.

Mrs. M.C. Nicolson,
Kirkby Wharfe,
Todcastle,
Yorkshire,
England.

Dear Mrs. Nicolson,

In reply to your Airletter received here on 25 May, I deeply regret to inform you that your husband was, in fact, killed while flying in this theatre. The circumstances are set out in the account of his death which we published in SEAC dated 27th May. I enclose a copy.

May I offer you my sincere condolences in your great loss? I have met several people out here who knew your husband, and all spoke highly of him. I regret that I myself never met him.

Yours faithfully,

Len Jackson
Lt.Cdr, RNVR.

EDITOR.

LJ/C.

Loss of kin notice.

RECORD OF SERVICE

OF

WING COMMANDER JAMES BRINDLEY NICOLSON VC DFC (39329)
DATE AND PLACE OF BIRTH: 29 April 1917, Hampstead

PREVIOUS SERVICE

Lance Corporal, Tonbridge School Officers Training Corps	1930-34

APPOINTMENTS AND PROMOTIONS

Granted a four year short service commission as an Acting Pilot Officer on probation in the General Duties Branch of the Royal Air Force (with effect from 12 Oct 36)	21 Dec 36
Confirmed in appointment and graded as Pilot Officer	12 Oct 37
Short service commission extended to six years Flying Officer	12 May 39
Acting Flight Lieutenant	1 Jun 40
Relinquished Acting Flight Lieutenant	16 Aug 40
Flight Lieutenant	3 Sep 40
Acting Squadron Leader (paid)	13 Mar 41
Retains Acting Squadron Leader	22 Sep 41
Acting Wing Commander	17 Mar 42
Squadron Leader	17 Jun 42
Transferred to the Reserve and retained on Active List	12 Oct 42
Retains Acting Wing Commander	Date unrecorded
Retains Acting Wing Commander	6 Jun 44
Relinquished Acting Wing Commander	23 Apr 45
Death presumed	2 May 45

POSTINGS

Civilian Flying School, White Waltham	12 Oct 36
Depot, 24 (Training) Group	21 Dec 36
No 10 Flying Training School, flying training	16 Jan 37
No 72 (Fighter) Squadron, flying duties	7 Aug 37
No 249 Squadron, flying duties	15 May 40
Station Boscombe Down, supernumerary	16 Aug 40
No 54 Operational Training Unit, chief ground instructor, operational training	24 Feb 41
Station Coltishall, supernumerary	15 Sep 41

No 1459 Flight flying duties	22 Sep 41
Headquarters, 293 Wing, India, flying duties	17 Mar 42
Station Alipore, to command	15 May 42
Station Raueli, Wing Liaison Officer	10 Oct 42
No 171 Wing, supernumerary	25 Nov 42
Air Headquarters, Bengal, training	16 Dec 42
No 27 Squadron	Date unrecorded
3rd Tactical Air Force, Allied Command South East Asia, training and tactics	6 Jun 44
Headquarters Royal Air Force Bengal/Burma, training/supernumary	4 Dec 44
No 355 Squadron	Date unrecorded
Missing believed killed following flying battle, death presumed	2 May 45

HONOURS AND AWARDS

Victoria Cross, London Gazette	15 Nov 40
Distinguished Flying Cross, London Gazette	11 Aug 44

MEDALS

1939-45 Star
Battle of Britain Clasp
Aircrew Europe Star
Burma Star
Defence Medal
War Medal 1939-45

The only Battle of Britain Victoria Cross, awarded to Flight-Lieutenant James Brindley Nicolson, together with his Distinguished Flying Cross and campaign service medals.

VC1O aircraft honouring Nicolson

The unveiling ceremony by Adur Council

Commemoration at Mullards 1970

Commemoration stone at Mullards

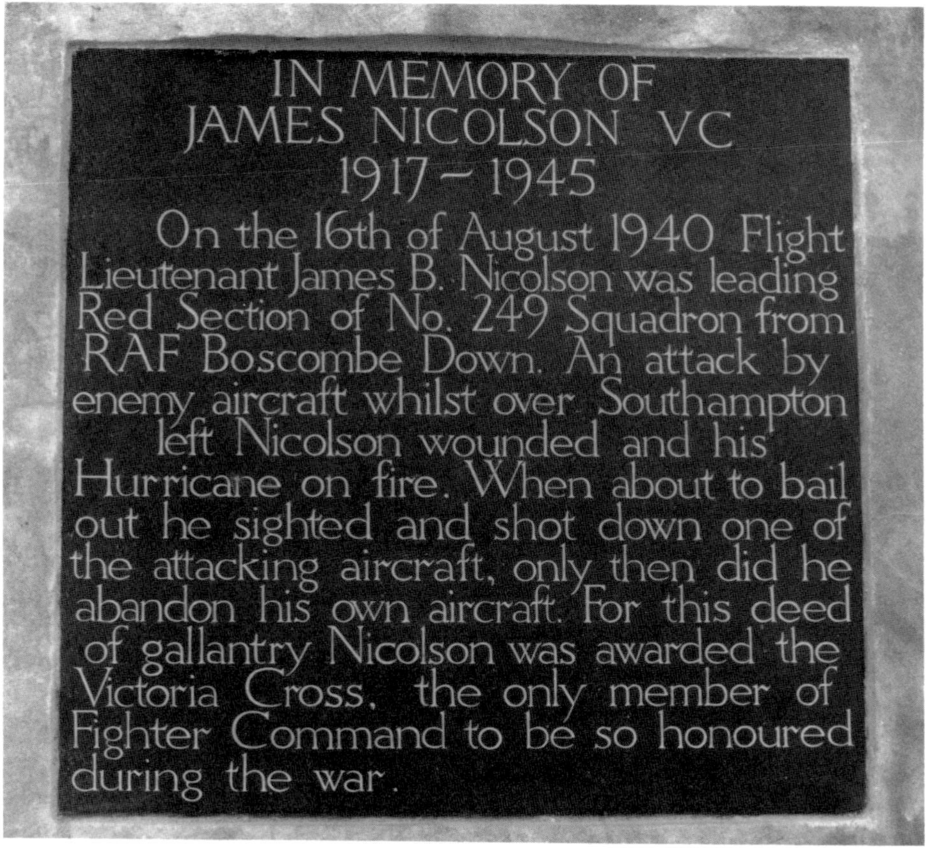

IN MEMORY OF
JAMES NICOLSON VC
1917 – 1945
On the 16th of August 1940 Flight Lieutenant James B. Nicolson was leading Red Section of No. 249 Squadron from RAF Boscombe Down. An attack by enemy aircraft whilst over Southampton left Nicolson wounded and his Hurricane on fire. When about to bail out he sighted and shot down one of the attacking aircraft, only then did he abandon his own aircraft. For this deed of gallantry Nicolson was awarded the Victoria Cross, the only member of Fighter Command to be so honoured during the war.

Commemorative plaque at Boscombe Down.

Nick's sister Jeanne with Wing Commander Neil at commemoration, Boscombe Down, 1990

72 Squadron —a brief history

The Badge

The badge displays a Swift volant —with the single motto 'Swift'.

Squadron history

The squadron was formed on 2 July 1917 from a nucleus detached from the Central Flying School. It left for Mesopotamia in December and inaugurated as a unit at Basra on 2 March 1918, equipped with a variety of aircraft. It was soon to be split up into smaller units and detached to the army, deployed in protection and tactical reconnaissance duties. Shortly after the war, the squadron reassembled in Baghdad where it was reduced to a cadre, and in February 1919 returned to England where it was disbanded on 22 September of that year.

At Tangmere on 22 February 1937, the squadron was reactivated in the fighter role, known as No 72(F), the aircraft on charge being Gladiators Mk 1 and detailed for duty at Church Fenton where it arrived on 1 June 1937 (see chapter two). April 1939 saw the first of the new Spitfires Mk 1 arrive, gradually replacing the doughty Gladiators, deployed on defensive duties on the east coast until June 1940, when it moved south to take part in the Battle of Britain and help cover the Dunkirk evacuation. Fighter sweeps over France commenced in July 1941 and on 8 November 1942 left for duty in North Africa operating from Gibraltar until airfields had been captured in Algeria. During the Tunisian campaign the squadron was engaged in bomber escort and fighter patrols and in June 1943 moved to Malta for offensive sweeps over Sicily. Following Allied landings in July and the subsequent capture of airfields on the island, 72 moved there followed by a further move to Italy. In July, 1944 they operated with a force of Spitfire squadrons in Corsica covering the landings in southern France in August, subsequently operating from France before returning to the Italian theatre. After further operations on ground attack sorties and defensive patrols until the termination of the war, the squadron sustained a spell of duty in Italy and Austria, and disbanded on 30 December 1946.

On 1 February 1947, No 130 Squadron at Odiham was renumbered 72 Squadron flying Vampires Fl and F3, later converting to Meteors F8, NF12, NF14 and Javelin FAW 4 and 5. On 15 November 1961 the squadron was again reformed at Odiham with Belvedere helicopters for transport support duties with No 38 Group, Transport Command. The Belvederes were exchanged for Wessexes in August 1964. The squadron headquarters are now at Aldergrove Northern Ireland.

No 249 Squadron the history

The badge

In front of a bezant, an elephant passant.

Motto

Pugnis et cacibus (With fists and heels)

Formed at Dundee in August 1918, the squadron was engaged in anti-submarine warfare off the Scottish coast until disbandment in October 1919. As related in chapter three, the squadron reformed at Church Fenton in May 1940 equipped with Spitfires, later Hurricanes. The first of the enemy aircraft destroyed — a Junkers 88 bomber — shot down on 8 July 1940.

The unit moved to Boscombe Down on 14 July 1940, to participate in the massed air onslaught by the Luftwaffe then waging. Throughout the Battle of Britain, 249 maintained a front line position against the Nazi hordes, based at Boscombe Down, and later at North Weald until May 1940. It was at this period that the squadron was given the title of 'Gold Coast Squadron'.

In May 1941, the squadron arrived at Takali in Malta and took part in the defence of the island, where, in March 1942 they re-equipped with Hurricane Mk II aircraft. On 18 May 1942 eight Spitfires were flown off an aircraft carrier to join the squadron at Takali.

The following few months saw the battle for supremacy over the island, the increase in enemy air attacks and their subsequent reduction. During this period the squadron was subjected to frequent air attacks, both on the ground and in the air, causing great damage to the aerodrome and buildings — and to aircraft. During May of 1942 the squadron destroyed its 100th aircraft and in April 1943 a squadron pilot shot down Malta's 1000th aircraft.

In the opening months of 1943, numerous targets in the Mediterranean, including harbour installations, a chemical factory and a power station were attacked. Returning from one of these operations, a surfaced enemy submarine, with its hatch open, was attacked and probably destroyed. With the invasion of Sicily on 10 July, and the subsequent shift of operations northwards, the squadron operated from Italy carrying out anti-shipping strikes on transport along the Yugoslav-Albanian coast, and operations in support of the Yugoslav partisans.

On 15 July 1944 the squadron was transferred to the Balkan Air Force which had been formed to co-ordinate operations across the Adriatic. Now equipped with

Mustangs and going immediately into operation from Brindisi, the squadron had considerable success despite bad weather in September, their 'destruction tote' was 15 aircraft destroyed and 23 damaged, plus 38 oil trucks and 112 vehicles either destroyed or damaged. This score was almost entirely achieved in Greece where sections operated from advanced landing grounds well within enemy territory. This squadron was the first in the Royal Air Force to operate behind the enemy lines in this manner. This phase of the squadron's operations terminated with the last operational sortie on 6 May 1945. The squadron disbanded in Italy on 16 August 1945.

In October 1945 No 500 (County of Kent) Squadron assumed No 249 Squadron's number plate and moved to Eastleigh, Kenya, as a photographic survey unit equipped with Baltimores. These aircraft were replaced in March 1946 by Mosquito aircraft only to be disbanded once more at Habbaniya, Iraq.

The fourth reformation of the squadron took place in early 1947, this time with Tempest fighter-bombers at Habbaniya. In 1950 it re-equipped with Vampire aircraft to be replaced by Venoms in 1955, and the squadron saw service at Deversoir, Ramat David, Shaibah, Amman, Nicosia, Akrotiri, Takali, El Adam, Aden and Sharjah.

249 went to war again briefly in November 1956, when it took part in the ground attack operations aimed at neutralising the Egyptian Air Force and anti-aircraft defences before the Allied paradrop at Gamil. Amongst the Egyptian war material the squadron claimed to have destroyed on the ground during these operations were 15 MIG-15's and five other aircraft and other war materials. The squadron lost no aircrew and only superficial damage sustained to their Venoms.

A few months later half the squadron then based at Eastleighmoved to Sharjah to operate against the Imam rebels in the Trucial States. A number of cannon and rocket sorties were carried out against the rebels, in support of the forces (led by the Sultan of Oman) who were engaged in neutralising the rebel-held forts and towers.

In October 1957 No 247 was disbanded yet again but reformed this time with Canberra light bombers, based at Akrotiri. After twelve years in the area being called upon to execute a variety of duties at any time, the squadron proved its continuance in the tradition which had been handed down since 1918. The squadron was disbanded for the last time on 24 February 1969

No 27 Squadron

The Badge

The badge depicts an elephant, the nickname given to the Martynside Scout which was the first aircraft used by the Squadron when it went to France in 1916.

Motto

QUAM CLERRIME AD ASTRA — can be translated 'With all speed to the Stars'

Squadron history

Since its formation in 1915 No 27 Squadron can truly claim to have one of the most exciting histories of any squadron in the Royal Air Force. It has operated in almost every major conflict to which the Service owes its tradition and has been active in a wide variety of roles — fighter, bomber, reconnaissance, transport and development flying.

In March 1916 the squadron took its 'Elephants' to France. Initially it was engaged in the fighter role but was eventually switched to long range bombing and reconnaissance. It operated in support of the war's major battles including the Somme, Ypres and Amiens, as well as carrying out successful raids on Zeppelin sheds. During this period it was also responsible for two outstanding pieces of development flying, namely high altitude reconnaissance and all-weather flying. The squadron was disbanded in England in January 1920 but in April of the same year was reformed in India. For many years it was engaged in operations against the notorious tribes of the North West Frontier and was rarely inactive until 1939 when, at the outbreak of war, it became a training unit at Risalpur.

In February 1941 the Squadron moved to Singapore and then to Malaya, but was unfortunately wiped out when the Japanese overran the island, but many of its personnel escaped to India by devious routes. There the squadron was again reformed and in December 1942 returned to action. It was the first squadron in the Far Eastern theatre to be equipped with the Beaufighter, its quiet engines were a prelude to such devastating attacks that it soon became known as 'the whispering death'. The many attacks carried out on enemy tactical targets included the destruction of half a million gallons of oil involving only two aircraft. In March 1945 the squadron was involved in air jungle rescue and supply dropping, and participated in special missions in support of clandestine forces.

After the war the squadron was disbanded but reformed again in 1947 as a transport squadron flying Dakotas, based in the United Kingdom, rendering good service in the saga of the Berlin airlift in 1948, after which it was soon disbanded.

On 1 April 1953 it was again reformed at RAF Scampton. Re-equipped with Canberra twin jet bombers it took part in demonstrations and goodwill visits to countries throughout Europe and the Mediterranean. In 1956 while based at Cyprus it was engaged in bombing sorties against Egyptian targets during the Suez crisis. In January 1957 the squadron returned to the UK and was disbanded yet again.

On 1 April 1961, the Squadron again reformed — for the second time at Scampton — equipped with the Vulcan Mk 2 as part of the first wing to use the Blue Steel stand-off bombs. The squadron was again disbanded in March 1972, but reactivated in November 1973 at RAF Waddington, for strategic reconnaissance duties with Vulcans, where it formed part of the front-line strength as the RAF's only full time medium strength maritime radar reconnaissance (MRR) squadron. Surveillance sorties were flown in an area stretching from the North Cape down to the Mediterranean, locating, shadowing and photographing Soviet shipping. The squadron was also used to direct simulated attacks by friendly aircraft on NATO shipping, and to patrol oil rigs and shipping within UK waters. During this period squadron personnel were often frequently detached to American bases to assist SAC B52 crews who were in the MR role. However the squadron was again disbanded in March 1982, amidst fears that this would be for the last time. Nevertheless, it was chosen as third UK Tornado Squadron and reformed at RAF Marham in May 1982 and operated in the all-weather role of strike attack, principally in the European theatre.

AIRCRAFT FLOWN

AIRCRAFT	ENGINE	~~AIRCRAFT~~ Aerodromes Visited	ENGINE	~~AIRCRAFT~~ Aerodromes Visited
D.H. 82.(a).	Gipsy Major	White Waltham		Duxford.
Hart.	Kestrel X	Hatfield.	Acklington	Catfoss.
Audax.	Kestrel X	Yatesbury.	Drem *	Ringway.
Tutor.	Cheetah	Sywell.	Abbotsinch	Tangmere
Fury.	Kestrel 2.S.	Ternhill.	Eastleigh	WITTERING.
Gladiator	Mercury IX	Netheravon	Shawbury.	Hemswell
Demon. D.C.	Kestrel 2S	Grantham.	Kirkbride	Leconfield.
Blenheim.	Mercury IX	Peterboro	Northolt.	Driffield
Magister.	Gipsy Major.	Sutton Bridge	West Hartford	Linton-on-Ouse
Hind.	Kestrel V.	West Freugh	Worthy Down	Dishforth
HARROW	PEGASUS XX	Church Fenton	North Weald	Hucknall
HEYFORD	KESTREL	Blackpool.	Boscombe Down	Digby.
Battle	Merlin II	Sealand.	Andover	Turnhouse
Spitfire	Merlin II	Catterick.	Hornchurch	Tollerton
Vega Gull.	Gipsy VI	Castle Bromwich	Brize Norton	Nostell Priory
Anson	Cheetah	Scampton	Hunsdon.	Biggin Hill.
Master	Kestrel XXX	Shoreham	Hibaldstow	Benson.
Hurricane	Merlin II	Feltwell.	Heston.	Abingdon.
Hurricane C.S.	Merlin III	Mildenhall.		Harwell
Gladiator 3 Blader	Mercury VIII	Farnboro'		Gullane*
Gladiator C.S.	Mercury IX	Hullavington		Manby.
Oxford.		Martlesham.		Elmdon
Boston		Aldergrove.		Derby.
Havoc I.		Cranwell.		Filton.
Owlet.		Waddington		

Whitney Straight.

Aircraft flown by Flight Lieutenant J. B. Nicolson

Tiger Moth

Source: Air Portraits

Avro Tutor Trainer

Source: Shuttleworth Collection

Miles Magister

Source: Air Photo Supply

Hawker Hart

Avro Anson

Hurricane Mk II

Source: Air Photo Supply

Source: Imperial War Museum

Bristol Beaufighter

de-Havilland Mosquito

EMP

MINISTRY OF INFORMATION,
MALET ST., W.C.1.

11th March, 1941.

Dear Flight Lieutenant Nicholson,

Chief Whirling Thunder of the "Indian Council Fire", a Society of American Indians with headquarters at Chicago, has sent to our Embassy in Washington eleven Eagle's Feathers asking that they may be presented to members of the Royal Air Force who have specially distinguished themselves in operations against the enemy, as marks of esteem from their Indian admirers across the Atlantic.

This friendly gesture is greatly appreciated by the British Government and the Air Ministry has asked this Ministry to give effect to the request of the "Indian Council Fire".

It has been decided that these Eagle's Feathers shall be presented to personnel awarded decorations in order of seniority.

I have pleasure therefore, on behalf of the "Indian Council Fire" in presenting you with this Eagle's Feather which it is hoped you will accept as a token of their esteem.

Yours sincerely,

Sir Walter Monckton, K.C.V.O.,K.C.,M.C.
Director-General

Flight Lieutenant J.B.Nicholson, V.C.

Red Indian Tribute to James Nicolson

Nicolson's son James holds a photograph of his father

REFERENCE INDEX

Acklington, 12, 32, 73
Aldbrough, 33
Archbishop of York, Dr Temple, 55
Atcherley, Wg Cdr, RLC, DFC, 72
Attlee, Major C. R., 56

Bader, D., 71
Bainton, Sgt, 91
Ball, A., 36
Ball, FO, 91
Bandon, Earl of, 2
Barton, Flt Lt, 32, 35, 128
Beamish, Sqn Ldr V., 11, 51, 52
Beaufighter, 72, 73, 78, 80, 81, 84, 87, 88, 94, 95, 96, 98, 127, 129
Beazley, PO, 33, 132
Bell, Sgt R., 119
Bladsworth, Mrs, 55
Blenheim, 16, 72, 80
Boscombe Down, 34, 35, 39, 43, 128, 132
Bourne, Flt Lt, 81
Bowhill, 52
Brewster Buffalo, 77
Briffett, PO, 84
British Schneider Trophy racing team, 10
Brize Norton, 35, 132
Brown, Sister E., 39
Buchanan, Wg Cdr, 81

Calcutta, 77, 78, 80, 81
Caldwell, Mrs N., 33, 34
Calland, FO J., 119
Calshott, 42
Cameron, Flt Sgt D., 119
Campbell, Sir M., 1
Capel Cure, Rev R. C., 55
Catalina, 119
Catfoss, 34
Cattell, Flt Lt, 3
Chippendale, Sgt, 94
Church Fenton, 9, 11, 12, 13, 31, 33, 34, 35, 71, 72, 82, 128, 134, 135
Churchill, W. S., 56, 127
Clough, Sgt, 84
Cobb, Mr T. C., 1
Coleman, Supt E., 40, 132
Collingwood, Sgt, 91
Crespigny, Gp Capt C. de, 82
Crombie, FO, 78
Curtiss Tomahawk, 77

Daish, Wg Cmdr H. C., 80, 81, 82, 84, 88, 117
Dakota 78, 82, 98
de Havilland School of Flying, 2
de Souza, Wg Cdr, G., 118, 119
Defiant, 72
Demon I, 11
Digby, 11
Dinwoodie, Flt Lt, 84, 91, 97
Dobbie, Alderman, 56
Dobson, FO, 95
Dodd, Sgt, 84
Doherty, Flt Sgt S., 119
Douglas DB-7 Havoc II, 72
Douglas, Sir S., 73
Douthwaite, Sgt B, 13
Dowding, AM Sir H., 11, 52, 71
Drem, 10, 13
Dukes, Mr E. A., 132
Dundee, 31
Duxford, 11

Eagle, Sgt. 13
Elsdon, FO T. A. F., 12, 82, 135
ENSA, 83
Ensor Sgt. 84
Exeter, 35, 73

Fairclough, FO, 95
Finingley, 73
Flamborough Head 34
Fleet Air Arm, 35
Franklin, Flt Lt 94, 95, 97, 127

Garland, FO, 52
General Electric Co, 72
Gillis, Sir H., 41
Gloster Gauntlet, 9
Gloster Gladiator, 9, 10, 11, 12, 13, 16, 135
Gosport, 35, 42
Gossage, AM, E. L., 52
Grandy, Marshal of the RAF Sir J., 31, 32, 34, 35, 42, 43, 55, 128, 133
Graves, C., 54
Gray, Sgt, 52
Grosvenor Hotel, 57

Halton, 41, 43, 51
Hamlyn, Sgt, 13
Hannah, Sgt, 52
Harkness, Flt Sgt B., 97
Harlow, H., 55
Hassell, FO, 91
Hawker Hart, 80
Hayr, AM, 118
Helmore, Wg Cdr, W., 72
Helsby, Sgt R., 119
Henstock, PO, 12, 13
Herbert, FO, 91
Heywood, Sgt, 84
Hibaldstowe, 72, 73
Hicks, Mr G., 56
Hill, FO B., 119
His Majesty King George VI, 56
Holmes, A., 55
Hope, Sqn Ldr E. J. L., 10, 11
Horn, Sqn Ldr E. B., 94, 97
Horsman, Ald. W., 56
Hull, 34
Humphries, Sgt, 91
Hunsdon, 73
Hurricane, 32, 33, 34, 35, 39, 42, 43, 44, 73, 77, 80, 98

Illingworth, Sqn Ldr, DFC, 84
Imperial Airways, 13, 34
Innes, Flt Lt D., 83, 91, 97, 129

Jagger, Sister B., 41
Johnson, Sgt, 84, 91
Johnston, PO, DFM, 97

Kellett, Flt Lt, 32, 34
Kent, Gp Capt HRH The Duke of, 43
Kightley, Flt Sgt E., 119, 120
King, PO, MA, 35, 36, 42
King, Sqn Ldr E. B., 35, 39, 43
Kingsley Wood, Rt Hon Sir, 16
Kirkby Wharfe, 10, 12, 39, 54, 55, 56, 72, 87, 137
Kirton Lindsey, 72
Kitchen, Miss M, 56

LDV, 40
Learoyd, Flt Lt, 52
Leconfield, 13, 35
Lee on Solent, 35
Leeds, 73
Lees, Sqn Ldr, 11, 13, 41
Liberator, 117, 118, 119, 120, 127
Lynn, V., 83
Lysander, 17

Mabey, Mr B. G., 1
MacIndoe, Sir A., 41
Magister, 72
Main, Sgt, 33
Mangan, WO, 135
Mannock, M, 36
Martin, Wg Cdr, 118
Mathewson, Sgt, 91
McCudden, J, 36
McMichael, Flt Lt, 84
McMichael, Wg Cdr J. H., 97
Meier, Oberlt, 33
Middle Wallop, 35
Millson, Sqn Ldr, 56
Mohawk, 82
Morris, Sqn Ldr, 56
Mosquito, 72, 73, 94, 95
Mountbatten, Lord L., 79, 91, 94, 118

Neil, PO T, 32, 35, 42, 127
Newall, ACM Sir C., GCB, CMG, CBE, AM, 16
Nicolson, Flt Sgt D., 119
No 3 Armament Training Corps, 3
No 27 Squadron, 80
No 72(F) Squadron, 12, 14, 16
No 151 Squadron, 39
No 213 Squadron, 11
No 224 Group Air Command, 80
No 303 Polish Squadron, 34
Norfolk, Sgt, 13
Norwich, 73
Nugent, Aircraftsman-2 R., 12

Observer Corps, 42
Orde, Capt C., 118
Osguthorpe, Sgt, 84
Oxland, Air Com, RD, 52

Palace Hotel, Torquay, 51, 54, 133
Palliser, Sgt Plt, 43
Park, AVM K., 52
Parnall, PO, 33
Pearl Harbour, 77, 78

Petch, Sgt, 84
Pharazyn, Flt Lt W. F., 12
Pierse, ACM Sir R., 78
Pigg, PO, 13
Pocock, Sgt, 13
Poole, 35
Portal, Lord, 52
Price, Cllr C. G., Mayor of Torquay, 54
Pring, Flt Sgt, 78
Pullen, WO M., 119, 120

Rangoon, 77
Reeves, CI Capt, 2
Ricardo Engines, 2
Richardson, Wg Cmdr G. T., 11
Riley, Mrs A., 131
Riley-Smith Hall, Tadcaster, 10, 55
Riley-Smith, Mr. & Mrs. W., 55
Ringwood, 35
Robson, PO N. C. H., 13
Rochester, 35
Rodgers, Sqn Ldr, B. H., 11

Salter, Flt Sgt, G., BEM, 97
Saul, AVM R. E., MC, DFC, 72
Scarborough, 34
Shaw, Sgt, 95
Sheen, PO D., 12
Shortis, Sgt, 94
Sinclair, Sir A., 44, 56
Skeen, Flt Sgt, 95
Slim, Gen, 98
Smith, Flt Lt F. W. (Hiram), 10, 14, 43, 51, 56
Sorley, AM Sir R., 43
Southampton, 36, 39, 42, 54
Spillard, PO J., 119
Spitfires, 10, 12, 13, 16, 32, 33, 91, 98, 128, 134, 135
Stapleford, 39
Staples, Sgt, 13
Statham, Sqn Ldr, AFC, 84
Steere, Sgt. 13
Sterling, FO R. A., 97, 129
Strood, 39
Sturrock, FO, 84
Swann, Wg Cmdr, W. E., 11
Swift, Flt Lt, 83

Tadcaster, 10, 11, 55
Tangmere, 9, 35, 43
Thomas, Sgt, 84, 91
Thompson, Flt Lt, 94, 129
Thorogood, WO, 84, 88, 91, 95, 97, 117
Thunderbolt, 98
Tiger Moth, 80
Tonbridge School, 2, 55
Torquay, 51, 54, 56
Torrance, Flt Lt, 94
Townsend, PO J., 83, 84
Trudgeon, PO, 95

Ulleskelf, 55

Vengeances, 98
Ventnor, IOW, 35, 43
Villa, PO J. W., 13
Vincent, Sgt, 91

Walker, PO R. J., 13
Wallens, Wg Cdr R. W., DFC, 133
Wandless, PO, 84
Watson Hall, Mrs, 56
Wavell, FM the Viscount Lord and Lady, 78, 117
Welch, FO, 84, 88, 117
Wells, Sqn Ldr P. H. V., DFC, 128
West Malling, 73
Westhampnett, 35
Whitley DSO DFC, Gp Capt E. W., 2
Wilcox, PO, E. J., 13
Williams Flt Lt, 91
Williams, FO, 91
Wingate, Maj Gen Orde, 98
Wittering, 11
Wootton, Mr F., 118

Yardley Court Prep School, Tonbridge, 1
York, 56, 73